4,68

RE-ORIENTATIONS

Other books by Hugh Tinker

Ballot Box and Bayonet: People and Government in Emergent Asian
   Countries

India and Pakistan: A Political Analysis

The Union of Burma: A Study of the First Years of Independence

The Foundations of Local Self-Government in India, Pakistan and
   Burma

Hugh Tinker

RE-ORIENTATIONS

Essays on Asia in Transition

FREDERICK A. PRAEGER, *Publishers*
New York · Washington · London

FREDERICK A. PRAEGER, *Publishers*
111 Fourth Avenue, New York 3, N.Y. U.S.A.
77–79 Charlotte Street, London, W.1, England

Published in the United States of America in 1965
by Frederick A. Praeger, Inc., Publishers

© Hugh Tinker 1965

Library of Congress Catalog Card Number: 65–19423

Printed in the United Kingdom

To Michael Argles

For thirty years of friendship

And when we clear away
  All this debris of day-by-day experience,
What comes out to light, what is there of value
  Lasting from day to day?

Acknowledgement

Certain of these essays have appeared in *Eastern World*, *International Affairs*, *International Journal*, *World Justice*, *New Society*, and *Man, Race and Darwin* (edited by Philip Mason), Oxford University Press, London and New York. The quotation overleaf is from *Autumn Journal*, by Louis MacNeice, Faber & Faber, London; published in his *Collected Poems*, Oxford University Press, New York.

CONTENTS

Prelude

THE notion of putting together some occasional pieces and calling the compilation a book is more popular with authors than publishers. Few of us are able to embark on this proceeding in the same style of superlative swank with which Macaulay advertised his *Critical and Historical Essays*:

> The author of these Essays is so sensible of their defects that he has repeatedly refused to let them appear in a form which might seem to indicate that he thought them worthy of a permanent place in English literature. Nor would he now give his consent . . . if . . . he could make republication impossible. But, as they have been reprinted more than once in the United States, as many American copies have been imported into this country, and as a still larger importation is expected, he conceives that he cannot, in justice to the publishers . . . longer object to a measure which they consider as necessary to the protection of their rights. . . .

Few indeed must be the instances of publishers pleading for the right to reissue assorted periodical pieces! And few are the collections of essays which take their place alongside full-length works as the choicest examples of an author's skill. Notable among these are the collected essays of G. M. Young. These can be consumed entire, as one ingests one's way through a leisurely six-course dinner of different but equally delicious dishes—or they can be sampled at random, like a box of chocolates. But all too often the reader becomes uneasily aware that the fare offered—which may include some of the author's rarest work—is padded out with pieces which serve only as makeweights. These are the literary equivalent of those corners of the bottom layer of the chocolate box which are revealed as filled with paper shavings. Uneven in quality, lacking a true homogeneity, most collections of essays are soon forgotten.

The present volume arises from the author's belief—now to be put to the test—that he has occupied a peculiarly fortunate position on the side-lines, during a period when the transformation of Asia, and the techniques for measuring and recording this transformation, have been going through a phase of exceptional significance. Having been a very minor actor in the final episodes of the decline and fall of western imperialism, the author then found himself placed in an academic position of being more or less detached from the events of the post-imperial epilogue, yet well supplied to observe their denouement. The crush of events clearly represented some sort of pattern: but what pattern? The methods of analysis, and the historical precedents which one could apply to these problems were insufficient to explain what was happening. It was necessary for the observer to fashion his own tools as he went along, in order to try to create meaningful explanations.

In these circumstances—aptly illustrated by the Burmese proverbs: 'Strong currents one moment, slack water the next', 'First the hare was ahead, then the hound'—it was prudent to withhold judgement. Yet here were fascinating problems crying out to be recorded and analysed. The measured processes of academic authorship seemed to this writer to be inappropriate under these circumstances. There was a compulsion (for which a respectable academic case might be adduced) to put into print first an accurate description of what was happening, and second an attempt at a hypothesis of why it was happening. This, at any rate, was my reaction (if I may now drop the attempt at third person detachment). Long ago, my supervisor at Cambridge, Dr David Thomson, now Master of Sidney Sussex College, observed in conversation that dons as authors fall into two classes: those who write too little, and those who write too much. There is no *via media*.

By temperament I belong emphatically to the school of dons who write too much. My idea of heaven is to be sitting at my desk, writing about a subject in which I am closely interested and upon which I feel I have something to say. As my typewriter clatters happily away, my bliss is unconfined. Conversely, my idea of hell is a week in term when committees, classes, boards of studies, seminars, and still more committees, prevent me from ever settling down at my desk.

However, this word-drunk or typewriter-happy condition of mine is always tempered by remembering something said by Philip Mason when he was writing his famous history of the Indian Civil Service, *The Men Who Ruled India*. Modestly, he eschewed any claim to being a professional historian. But, he added, he could claim to be a professional writer. In composing *The Men Who Ruled India* he had at one stage written a draft of thirty thousand words—and then had thrown the draft away. 'Having written thirty thousand words, and then thrown them away, I think I can call myself a professional writer', he said. Hard words: especially to those for whom composition is not easy. But the message was impressed upon me, and I have always tried to be selective about my own writing. 'If in doubt, cut' is a good maxim. Nevertheless, over the years, I have written a lot of what I would be content to describe as journalism, some of which still may have a place in the development of a literature of Asian studies. Then there have been the occasions—such as the delivery of an inaugural lecture as the first professor of Government and Politics with reference to Asia in the University of London—which have called for whatever is original in my thinking, but which have required ideas to be contained within a limited compass. And so I have presumed to gather together this selection of the writings of a decade. That I am able to offer them now in book form is due to the good fortune of my having as my friend a publisher who is primarily interested in living ideas, and not in some mechanical, dried-out formula for success.

Whatever value these essays possess arises from the ideas they seek to develop; these are 'think pieces', in the expressive American phrase. The overall purpose of this book is to show how one man's point of view changed, and perhaps developed, while being exposed to the pregnant happenings of the 1950s and early 1960s. It may not, therefore, be mere egotistical introspection which leads me to begin by defining what I regard as my own professional and personal standpoint.

A professor of Government and Politics is, I suppose, automatically categorised as a political scientist. Although this term is convenient shorthand to describe that place in university studies which is a kind of rallying-point for a number of disciplines (political philosophy, political history, constitutional law, sociology *et al.*) the connotations of 'political science' have never been acceptable to me as a description of what I conceive I am doing. This may be silly, subjective pedantry. *The Concise Oxford Dictionary* tells me that science is 'systematic and formulated knowledge'; and I can only hope that is what I am about in my study of Asian politics. But when the dictionary goes on to refine its definition as 'deductions from self-evident truths, as mathematics, logic' and 'one dealing with material phenomena and based mainly on observation, experiment, and induction, as chemistry, biology' then I know why I am uneasy. For political studies deal not with self-evident truths, but with human behaviour and human thought, in all its perplexity; while the phenomena which ought properly to be included within the ambit of politics are so vast and vague that nobody can observe and measure more than a fraction of the relevant evidence. Finally, the controlled conditions of experiment, though occasionally faked by some political scientists, are really unobtainable; in normal circumstances, the variables go far beyond the control of the observer. For good or ill, my viewpoint is expressed in words with which I closed a review of a work by a leading American 'behavioural' political scientist: 'Academic students of politics are not detached spectators, surveying a slide under the microscope: we are down there among the amoebae, wriggling with all the rest.'[1]

It is the climate and character of the scholar's outlook which delimits the quality of his scholarship. Whether the scholar is a Marxist or a Liberal; an American, Englishman, or Indian; whether he is a Buddhist or a Baptist; whether he was born in 1880 or 1910 or 1940; whether he plays chess or poker: all these are factors which contribute towards the conclusions he will reach on any given problem, no matter how much his professional training may have impressed upon him the importance of objectivity.

Because I see the student of any aspect of human activity as

[1] *Journal of Asian Studies*, Vol. XXII, No. 3, 1963, p. 337.

himself a part of the subject he seeks to observe, I find it much easier to adapt the description of 'historian' to the kind of study in which I am engaged than that of political scientist. Academic historians are inclined to differentiate themselves from political scientists by reference to the nature of their source materials. An historian is one who studies documents, according to this view. But to my way of thinking, the most acceptable concept of history is that of R. G. Collingwood, interpreting Benedetto Croce: 'The conscious-ness of one's own activity as one actually performs it. History is thus the self-knowledge of the living mind.' This is really only a more abstract expression of G. M. Young's dictum: 'Go on reading until you hear people talking. Then you will understand why things happened as they did.'[2] Collingwood observes that: 'Historical knowledge is not concerned only with a remote past', and 'the so-called science of human nature or of the human mind resolves itself into history'. And so, he concludes: 'The *Republic* of Plato is an account, not of the unchanging ideal of political life, but of the Greek ideal as Plato received it and re-interpreted it.... Hobbes's *Leviathan* expounds the political ideas of seventeenth-century absolutism in their English form. Kant's ethical theory expresses the moral convictions of German pietism.'[3]

Where these giants emerge as mirrors of their own age, why should we little people seek to assert more than that we are the reflection of the attitudes of our own day? Yet some contemporary political scientists see fit to claim that they are endowed with a new and total vision of the nature of politics. The foreword to Almond and Coleman's *Politics of the Developing Areas* asserts: 'This book sets out to do two things. The first is to construct a theoretical framework that makes possible, for the first time, a comparative method of analysis for political systems of all kinds.'[4] This grandiose contention is followed by a re-hash of commonplace mid twentieth-century transatlantic orthodoxy: an almost complete example of the mind enslaved by its environment.

Surely, the most that the observer of politics can attain—being

[2] G. M. Young, *Today and Yesterday*, London, 1948, p. 112.

[3] R. G. Collingwood, *The Idea of History*, Oxford, 1946, esp. pp. 202, 219–29.

[4] G. A. Almond and J. A. S. Coleman, *The Politics of the Developing Areas*, Princeton, 1960, p. v.

himself a mirror of his age—is to hold up a mirror to contemporary events which does not distort or deflect the picture which it is reflecting? In choosing a description for my own kind of writing I am quite content to be regarded as a specialised journalist with a detached point of view (what else was Daniel Defoe?). Yet if I must aspire to a more academic label I would ask to be called a contemporary historian.

During the period when the great *Civil Histories* of the second world war were appearing under the editorship of Sir Keith Hancock, the role of contemporary history, as such, seemed to have become established. In the early 1950s, some of us used to meet in a seminar directed by Sir Keith (one of the few academic exercises which I look back to with nostalgia as a formative experience of an astringent yet exhilarating kind). It then appeared as though a vigorous school of contemporary historians would be established to foster 'the continuous assertion of a past which is not past and of a present which is not present', 'the formulation of experience as a whole'.[5] This did not come about. The term, 'contemporary history', fell into desuetude, and we all had to make the artificial choice of becoming political scientists, or of remaining historians: or, in my case, of trying to be some sort of hybrid, regarded as at best a well-meaning agnostic by the devout of both sects.

However, a contemporary historian I remain. Looking back at the minutes of one of those Hancock seminars, I note that we gave consideration to Thucydides as 'a contemporary historian who had surmounted a natural bias'; so perhaps I had better devote the remainder of this Prelude to some account of the various fluctuations which have occurred in my own natural bias, and relate these to the subject-matter of this book.

There are some scholars who appear to attain a fusion with their subject in their undergraduate or graduate phase, which enables them to shine with a pure clear light for the remainder of their academic lives undisturbed by the gusts and vapours of the times. I am well aware that I have only proved able to delineate my present point of view in the light of the kaleidoscope of circumstance through which I have passed during a quarter of a century.

[5] Michael Oakeshott, *Experience and its Modes*, Cambridge, 1933, p. 111.

6

Unlike most academics, I was plunged into the 'university of life' at an early age. Soon after I was seventeen, I went to work as a very junior local government officer in the old metropolitan borough of St Pancras. As I write, St Pancras is being submerged in the new synthetic borough of Camden; so there is no harm in saying that if the local government I saw from the nether side was not altogether Old Corruption, it was not exactly reformed either. The spirit of 'Lucky Jim' prevailed. Everything was makeshift (even now, I still drive each week past our old 'temporary' library in Camden Street, opened before the first world war). Was my experience unique? I do not know. Certainly, no other local authority can ever have had a member of the Library Committee like Councillor Krishna Menon. As I said in a recent review: 'Upon a youth of seventeen he made an indelible impression—not then as an Indian nationalist, but as a human personality—erratic, sometimes scarifying, but always compelling.'

In those days, I was an obsessive reader (I consumed more books in a month, at seventeen, than I do now in a year). Among all the others, I read books about local government. I was astonished. Of course there was a general similarity between the operations described by Jennings and Laski and those in which I was immersed: but there was a great deal which seemed to have escaped the notice of these observant scholars. From that time, the relation between appearance and reality has always been of prime importance to me. Truth so often seems to be wrapped up inside several layers which must be peeled away before one comes upon reality. Years later, when I was set to read the great masters of political thought, I was awed by their profundity—but only when I came to *Human Nature in Politics* by Graham Wallas was I moved to exclaim: 'Yes, this man knows things as they are.'

As an observer, then, I have always tried to understand the *context* of the thought or action, and to distinguish between how things are, and how they ought to be. My perhaps excessive suspicion of the present fashion for 'model building' in the social sciences arises from the conviction that, in nine cases out of ten, the theoretical model comes first, and the evidence is then introduced to illustrate its validity: instead of an exhaustive study of the evidence preceding the tentative construction of the model.

Having acquired this awareness of the possible variation be-

7

tween appearance and reality, the fortunes of war led me to volunteer for the Indian Army. Little has changed about the physical surroundings of the India Office since that day in 1940 when I first walked up Clive Steps and through those gloomy doors into the ante-chamber to India: that India which has been my life and my inspiration. Today, the India Office may be partitioned between parvenu departments: but the personality of Victorian India still dominates those lofty corridors and staircases. In a radio talk, a few years ago, I described the India Office library as it still is today: 'Here it seems as if time called a halt about the year of Queen Victoria's first Jubilee. Everything is old and worn and very still. A clock ticks wearily. Even Big Ben's booming is muffled. Pens scratch busily. And behind barricades of fat, heavy, leather-bound volumes sit the students. Most are from India and Pakistan. A few are Burmese and Chinese. Over in the corner is a retired general. A few seats away, a former High Court Judge. The common bond that unites them all is a love of Asia and the scholar's desire for knowledge.' This is the last remnant of the India Office today: but when I first entered those doors, it was the communications centre of the greatest imperial possession on earth.

How different everything was in 1940! Will the reader believe me when I recall that the jolly old Indian Army colonel who saw me ended our interview with the advice: 'Whatever you do, take a well-cut pair of riding breeches and a dinner jacket'? Between my nineteenth and twenty-fifth years, I played my little walk-on role in the final and perhaps the finest hour of the old Indian Army and the old Indian Civil Service. Did the last legionary who looked back at Hadrian's Wall realise that no Roman would ever again rule in Britain? We who saw the last weary British and Indian soldiers stagger out of Burma in April and May 1942 could not doubt that we were witnessing the end of an empire. What remained was to show that there was greatness still in the old tradition. The brief episode after the war of my service in the administration of the United Provinces was a glimpse through a door that was closing on what had been, and on what might have been.

When the British withdrawal made way for bloodshed, it seemed that the work of the administrators and soldiers was in ruins. The mood of that hour is commemorated in the biting words of an old Punjabi officer, contemplating the slaughter in the autumn of 1947: 'The British are a just people. They have left India in exactly the same state of chaos as they found it.'[6]

Then routine reasserted its balm. Things went on much as before: to those who had feared worse, what reassurance. Already, I had joined the School of Oriental and African Studies and had begun to teach history. What seemed important to me then was to emphasise continuity; to show how a partnership founded in an unequal relationship could be perpetuated on a firm foundation. As an example of my outlook in those early years of independence—the post-imperial epilogue—here are some passages from a BBC broadcast of 1953, in which I was reviewing the first volume of Philip Mason's *The Men Who Ruled India*, and Lord Birdwood's *A Continent Decides* (a book since undeservedly forgotten):

> As British officials and British soldiers left Karachi, Bombay, Calcutta and Rangoon in 1947 and 1948, associations which had been built up over two hundred years were abruptly terminated. The account was closed. A final black line was drawn across the ledger. And during the first years of independence, we in Britain have begun to add up the figures; to try and estimate the moral and spiritual profit and loss of British rule. But people here are hoping that the closing of the old ledger-book is to be followed by the opening of new accounts. India, Pakistan and Ceylon have elected to continue as members of the Commonwealth. They have chosen to adopt forms of parliamentary government which are English in origin. Most of the institutions which developed in the British period are flourishing today: such as the famous regiments of the armies of Pakistan and India, an independent judiciary, the universities, still employing English as a common tongue.
>
> This is the theme which runs through [Mason's and Birdwood's books]. . . . Both are linked by their desire to justify and maintain the comradeship of India and Pakistan with Britain. This is not just a matter of trade advantages or power politics, or of a proud nation clinging to its past glories; it is simply that the great continent which stretches from the Khyber to Cape Comorin has become a part of our thoughts and our lives.

[6] Quoted in R. Symonds, *The Making of Pakistan*, London, 1950, p. 74.

Almost every family in Britain has sent one or many of its members to that continent in the last two hundred years. In every parish church throughout England there are tablets recording the names of sons of the parish who rest in the earth of Peshawar or Allahabad or Bangalore or a hundred other cantonments of long ago. . . .

What will be the feelings of readers [of *The Men Who Ruled India*] in India and Pakistan? Some may feel irritated that Englishmen occupy so much of the stage, and others will think that the author has glossed over the more dubious activities of his countrymen (although he somewhat disarms potential criticism by insisting that 'men must be judged not by their worst but by their best'). Other readers, I fancy, will realise that this story is an episode in a partnership. For British rule in India was always more Indian than British . . . Up to 1858, the British were the senior partners; thereafter they became co-partners; until finally their Muslim and Hindu colleagues assumed full charge of the concern. This was a continuing tradition. As a small example, on Monday *The Times* contained an account of an interview with the chief secretary of Punjab, Mr Akhtar Hussain, who still keeps upon his walls the fading photographs of his British mid-Victorian predecessors. Here is an instance of a service which is greater than race or country.

Lord Birdwood, no doubt, would be regarded by most as a conservative; he calls himself 'an Englishman soaked in the associations of the past', and his book will come as a surprise to those Asians who still imagine that British conservatives wish to put the clock back to 1939. In his book there are no regrets, no harping back to bygone days. Instead there is a whole-hearted acceptance of the new era of independence, and a genuine interest in the future. . . . His central theme, one with which few will quarrel, is of the need for members of the Commonwealth to get to know each other: for the peoples of Asia and Africa, North America and the Pacific to meet and learn each other's special problems and ideas. In this he sees the principal hope of the Commonwealth achieving an organic unity of purpose and ideals.

Lord Birdwood himself comes from a family which, in Kipling's phrase, 'served India, generation after generation, as dolphins follow in line across the sea'.... There will continue to be a wide public in Britain for books such as these which keep alive old affections for some corner of India or Pakistan or Burma, and interpret their present-day activities with detachment yet with sympathy.

This mood of 1953 was, no doubt, superficial and sentimental. The emphasis upon partnership is one I am glad to remember, but which was to prove over-optimistic. Altogether, there was too much expectation that the new states would continue to function in the mould formed by the British; a facile assessment that, because parliament (for example) had continued for six years or so upon the correct Erskine May model, it was therefore firmly established in that pattern.

The emphasis which I was then placing upon continuity was, however, not shared by other liberally-minded observers. A more general feeling was that with independence, the new states had achieved a new birth of freedom. Liberation from colonial rule had solved all problems, political and economic, and started the new states off upon a new plane of endeavour. It was in this mood that a conference of historians, many coming from Asia, gathered together at the School of Oriental and African Studies in 1956. They devoted some considerable attention to indicating how racial or religious bias had distorted the outlook of western historians of times past, while proclaiming that, as the new men, they were now able to produce a version of history which would be objective and definitive. It was my view then, as now, that scholars are the creatures of time and place and the first essay which follows represents an attempt made in 1956 to assess the trends of contemporary historical writing on Asia as they reflected the changing pattern of the times.

The comforting asseveration, which I have quoted above, that British conservatives had no wish to put the clock back, was rudely destroyed by the Suez war of 1956. I was ashamed of the immorality and illegality of an act which seemed to me to reduce Britain to the level of a cynical aggressor. Part of the psychology of Suez was a hankering after the great days of the British Empire, and perhaps it was as an unconscious reaction against *folie de grandeur* that I now began to move away from my emphasis upon the theme of the relationship between Britain and India and her neighbours, and to view the political evolution of southern Asia as an autonomous development.

Those in Britain who sought to establish a frame of reference for modern Asian political studies in the 1950s found themselves trying to steer between the Scylla of traditional 'Orientalism', and the Charybdis of Europe-centric studies. The dilemma was posed in the opening passage of an article of mine in *Pacific Affairs*:

For some Asian specialists, the most discouraging label that can be tied around their necks is that of 'Orientalist'. The name raises the vision of an ancient in skull-cap, with spectacles awry, poring over an obscure inscription in an obscure script in an obscure language (Sogdian, most probably). Oriental History, Oriental Languages: these fall into separate water-tight compartments divorced from the normal study of history or language. The normal focus of humane studies is assumed to be the West. For example, in the History School of the University of London—probably the most enterprising in Britain—there are seven branches of study. Branches iii to vii comprise South Asia, the Near and Middle East, East and South-East Asia, Eastern Europe, and Africa. Branch ii is simply called 'Medieval and Modern History'. It is in fact the history of western Europe, but in the minds of the majority of British historians western European history and history, *tout court*, are synonymous. . . .

Perhaps there is a chicken and egg aspect to this situation; young scholars are reluctant to enter fields where, they surmise, standards of scholarship are lagging behind. Certainly a historian would be compelled to acknowledge that both in technical craftsmanship and in intellectual development Asian historical work is at least fifty years behind that of some other areas. . . .

Things look most hopeful in the discipline of political thought and government. During the last five years there has been much original work, but this has been addressed mainly to fellow specialists in the area and has not reached a wider academic audience. When will Asian political studies produce a Bagehot or de Tocqueville, someone who illuminates the whole subject? The impact of democracy upon what are still medieval societies, in many ways, in Asia and Africa represents the biggest political upheaval in the political history of the world; yet thus far there have been no attempts at a general interpretation of the phenomenon.[7]

The dilemma which I have been trying to define consists in finding a basis for the study of Asian political development which will not relegate the study to the exotic plane of Orientalism, yet will not reduce Asian politics to an aspect, a sub-branch of western political studies. Indeed, as the passage above indicates, there is much in the rise of modern Asia which deserves recognition as having a special significance for the wider understanding of political thought and action.

The second essay, "The City in Asia", represents a considered effort to demonstrate the autonomous validity of Asian political studies. An approach to a political theme was chosen which has been generally ignored by political analysts (though adopted by some sociologists).

My growing awareness of the need to establish a basis for Asian studies which was neither 'Oriental' nor a branch of western study was combined with a sense that it was necessary to venture farther in finding the right 'level' of study. As I observed in the paper quoted above, emphasis in modern Asian historical studies in England (which very largely means studies at my own School) seemed to me to be misdirected. Here are my views, again formulated in a review of a work (B. B. Misra, *The Indian Middle Classes*) which to some extent breaks new ground:

Hitherto, [Indian historical studies] have concentrated upon diplomatic and administrative activity, especially in the sphere of what is called 'policy'. 'Policy' (it is usually assumed) can be determined by referring to the resolutions and minutes of secretaries of state and governors-general. This form of historical reconstruction is culled almost entirely from official and semi-official papers, correspondence and ordinances. A technique has been established in which the interaction of subject and material, material and subject, has been propelling Indian historical studies along a groove from which professional workers hardly ever attempt to emerge. . . .

The main impetus for the formation of a new middle class came from the enormous expansion of British rule. Traditional

[7] "Political Studies and the New Asia" in *Pacific Affairs*, September 1960, p. 300.

13

legal, literary and financial skills were adapted to the requirements of the new British administrative system: there was a
definite correlation between the old, literary Hindu upper castes
and the new, professional middle class. . . .

At different periods, different groups have played a dominant role, giving way to others: the Brahmo Samaj Bengalis in
the 1860s and 1870s, the Chitpavan Brahmans in the 1890s and
1900s, Gujaratis in the 1920s and 1930s, U.P. Brahmans from the
1920s onward: with the Malabaris as the present contenders for
eminence. When we understand the reasons for the ebb and
flow of power between castes and regions we shall know much
more about the general factors in the rise of the middle class.
Dr Misra largely ignores all this. . . . He introduces the Marwaris as *banyans* [agents], observing that they 'established a
pattern of behaviour at once timid and parsimonious'. His next
reference to the Marwaris [200 pages later] finds them in control of the most powerful industrial cartels in modern India!
How did this metamorphosis come about? Dr Misra advances
no explanation. One can hardly evade this as a sociological
question, outside the range of the historian: contemporary
British historians never stop talking about the rise (or fall) of
the gentry. But historians of India are not yet attuned to such
problems: they still try to tackle every question as a matter of
policy. . . . The difficulty of departing from the conventional
'policy' point of view is accentuated by the type of source
material which the author has chosen to use. This, too, is conventional: dispatches, parliamentary papers, reports of commissions and committees. No use is made of Indian material; not
even letters or memoirs; still less, newspapers, novels, drama,
or the family records which most upper castes maintain. . . .[8]

The concept of policy being made at the top level, or even of
government functioning exclusively at the top level, seemed to me
to provide a poor focus for historical or political studies. My own
first book was a study of the working of local self-government in

[8] *Bulletin of the School of Oriental and African Studies*, Vol. XXV,
Part 2, 1962, pp. 385–6. In fairness to Dr Misra it should be added that
the passages quoted above do less than full justice to the scope and depth
of his valuable study.

the Indian Empire in the late nineteenth and early twentieth centuries. In a modest style, the book set a trend in studies of the local community in its dealings with authority; an aspect which now receives equal academic 'parity of esteem' alongside studies of the higher echelons of government.

One of the most significant developments within recent years has been the recognition by leaders of all shades in the new states that governments must be rooted in the support of the ordinary folk, the little people, at their local level, if they are to acquire a genuinely national dynamism. As an example of the diversity of this subject, a comparative study, "Community Development: a New Philosopher's Stone?" is included.

In the late 1950s, western observers of Asian politics were given a succession of sharp and no doubt salutary warnings to be chary of complacency in assuming that western democratic institutions could be easily transplanted, without a period of acclimatisation in Asian soil. Writing in 1957, in a volume entitled *Democratic Institutions in the World Today*, I commented:

> The relationship of the military to government is not often examined by writers on law, politics, or constitutional theory, but a professional, reliable, non-political army is another component of democracy. Whenever an army takes upon itself the task of government and politics, the end is almost inevitably dictatorship and the stifling of all opposition, as in Kuomintang China, Peron's Argentina, or Nasser's Egypt. The idea of a non-political, professional army is not well established in world practice. Wellington's army was both amateur and involved in politics; the French and German armies were highly professional but, right up to the second world war, both attempted to play a part in politics.... No democracy has yet shown itself able to dispense with a reserve of armed force with which to maintain order in an emergency. Unless the army accepts an allegiance higher than that of governments and parties, a loyalty to the established law of the state, it will not be prepared to intervene—and then withdraw when normality is restored.[9]

[9] W. Burmeister (ed.), *Democratic Institutions in the World Today*, London and New York, 1958, pp. 129–30, Ch. vi, "Democratic Institutions in India and China".

So far I seem to have shown remarkable prescience: today, there are dozens of works by political scientists on the role of the military in politics, but in 1957 there were few.[10] However, it must be admitted that I did not appreciate the significance of one of the sentences quoted above ('Unless the army accepts an allegiance higher than that of governments and parties ...'). In 1958, General de Gaulle was recalled to power by the generals, employing precisely the argument that they were motivated by just such a higher loyalty. In 1957, I certainly did not anticipate the imminence of the military take-over in Pakistan. However, when in February and March 1958 I made my first visit to Pakistan since Partition, there could be no mistaking the omens. I remember, on my return, ringing up a member of the staff of the *Economist* and suggesting that I should contribute a piece. 'Pakistan looks all right, outwardly, but inwardly it is rotten', I said. My journalist friend replied: 'I don't even think Pakistan *looks* all right.' His words were soon confirmed by events.

An early attempt to assess the significance of the military revolutions in Asia was made in a BBC Third Programme talk, "Gunpowder in Asian Politics".[11] This was mainly concerned to analyse the background to the *coups*, stressing the warrior, *kshattriya* tradition in Asian society. The survey concluded:

It still remains true that in southern Asia the initiative in national leadership lies with a middle class that is civilian in outlook; trained in the universities and at the law.... All this provides a real basis for the nourishment of democracy which is almost totally lacking in the Middle East. There (outside Israel and Turkey) the authoritarian tradition of government is nowhere seriously questioned by a powerful professional middle class. But one cannot be complacent, even about Ceylon and India. Launching a military *coup* in the climate of Asian democracy today is rather like introducing smoking for girls into a strict Victorian family. The eldest daughter puffs her cigarette in agonies of conscience. The second feels daring too.

[10] For example, see S. E. Finer, *The Man on Horseback; the role of the military in politics*, London and New York, 1962. Finer's bibliography lists few works before the late 1950s, except for South America.

[11] See the *Listener*, December 11, 1958.

16

By the time the third and fourth are at it, smoking has become *de rigueur*. . . .

There is still no upsurge of military dictatorship in southern Asia. But the atmosphere is changing. Army commanders will no longer stand aside when politicians show themselves unworthy. In particular, if politicians attempt to meddle in purely military matters, or if they demonstrate that they are unable to preserve the fabric of law and order, there is likelihood of intervention. Where the army has descended into the political arena it will not find it so easy to withdraw to the old seat in the grandstand. Pakistan in particular may be in for an experience like that of Turkey under Ataturk. But belief in democracy in southern Asia should not be underrated. Performance may not have attained the ideal envisaged by enthusiasts before independence, but ten years is too short a time to transform attitudes shaped over centuries.

Some foreign observers are glad to see army rule. They admire the discipline, self-control and moderation of the army leaders. The senior officers of Pakistan, India, and Ceylon—so immaculately turned out, so genial, so redolent of all that is best in Sandhurst and Camberley—are particularly reassuring. But for my part I put my money on the less sartorially presentable Asian products of the London School of Economics. Conversation with one senior Asian army commander who had visited Communist China was particularly revealing. No flies, no offal, no pariah dogs. The trains all ran to time. In short, the people were all so obedient. No doubt it is an excellent thing that barracks shall be swept and whitewashed, and soldiers respond to the word of command with unified, automatic precision. But the warm-hearted peoples of southern Asia deserve a better fate than to inhabit one vast barrack square.

The tone of this analysis—sounding a warning that it was easier to start a military revolution than to see it through, and challenging the hasty assumption that democracy had 'failed' in the new states—was somewhat different from the conclusions of most western observers of Asia, whether professional journalists or university professors. Having too soon assumed that a new world had arisen in the 1940s, they now assumed (again too soon) that all had come crashing down in ruins at the end of the 1950s. My insistence that military take-overs did not provide a short-cut, being merely a variation on authoritarianism, and that parliamentary democracy (however imperfect) was the only genuine alternative to communist authoritarianism, was something I felt in my heart, as well as my head. The late 1950s were the chrysalis time of my transformation from passive liberal into active Liberal in politics. I cannot, and do not pretend that my academic observations remained immune from this process.

Among my attempts *c.* 1959 at taking a longer view of developments in Asia, one which appeared in *International Journal, a Canadian Quarterly*, is now reprinted: "Climacteric in Asia". Another effort to penetrate through the formalistic study of parliaments and political parties to fundamental influences in Asian government and society is my essay: "India today: A Nation in Making, or Breaking?", which originally appeared in the "Events and Trends" series which are a feature of the Belgian Catholic journal *Justice dans le Monde/World Justice*.

In the 1950s, the relationship between the West and the new states was being vitally affected by a factor which crept almost unnoticed into international relations: foreign aid. When President Kennedy announced on May 26, 1961, 'Foreign aid must become a full partner in American foreign policy', he set the seal on a process which had been maturing for a decade. Those concerned in the application of aid persisted for many years in regarding this as a technical, even a business operation, and ignored its political and cultural overtones. "The Name and Nature of Foreign Aid" was an early attempt to look beyond the immediate implications of aid. Even in the middle 1960s, there are some lessons still to be learned; in the late 1950s, there was an almost total lack of awareness that there was anything to be learnt about the side-effects of aid among the economists and other advisers who produced their nostrums so confidently, and with such odd effects.

The academic observer of Asia today has an advantage over his journalist colleagues—even those who are Asian specialists—in that he is better enabled 'to see life steadily and see it whole'. They are continually required to switch their gaze from one crisis in one state to the next crisis in the next state and, notoriously, no news cannot be news: whereas it is often the lacunae in Asian affairs which provide the *clou* to the whole panorama. Increasingly, to me, the key to understanding the drift of things in Asia was to be found in the nature of the relationship between governors and governed. The 'we' or 'they' aspect of government has now become a commonplace of political writing on Asia, but when I delivered my lecture to the Royal Historical Society, "People and Government in Southern Asia", in November 1958, this mode of assessing the impact of government had been little considered.[12]

The contemporary historian—if he is worth his salt—has to reconcile himself to his own individual insights of today becoming the commonplaces of tomorrow. For example, an article of mine, "New Lamps for Old", appeared in *International Affairs*, October 1960. This posed the question: 'How can the public services successfully bridge the difficult interregnum between colonial rule and complete independence?' I showed how the sudden withdrawal of British civil servants had come about in southern Asia largely by default of any positive planning to the contrary. I suggested how the anachronistic model of the Colonial Civil Service might be subsumed into a forward-looking Commonwealth Civil Service. And I drew attention to the total absence of nationals as trained officials (other than clerks and subordinates) in territories such as Uganda and British Borneo. Noting that 'as yet no urgent demand for self-government is asserted', I urged that 'it would be foolish not to recognise that within fifteen years all these will most probably enjoy some form of autonomy. If this stops short of independence, like the present [1960] status of Singapore, it will still be quite distinct from colonial rule. Now is the time to initiate training schemes in government. . . .'

There was nothing much wrong with my diagnosis: but how completely wrong I was in my time-table! Within three years, these territories in East Africa and in South-East Asia where 'no urgent demand for self-government is asserted' had been flung into independence by a British government bored with the responsibility of empire, and unwilling to run any risk of unpopularity, and perhaps obloquy. And so the established method of preparing for independence by first training officials and legislators in the techniques of administration and government was pushed aside, and indepen-

[12] Reprinted in *The Transactions of the Royal Historical Society*, 5th Series, Vol. 9, 1959.

dence was dumped (as it were) in the laps of the politicians of East Africa. My article ended:

> Only in time will the new political bosses discover that a supine, complacent bureaucracy cannot generate the dynamic which is required to implement plans for industrialisation, rural development and social betterment which are the dream of Africa and Asia. Instead, there will be delay, hesitation, passing the buck, an absence of creativity, such as obtains today in the working of the public services of Burma and Indonesia.... An efficient public service is not an infallible recipe for success for a new nation: but in the absence of such a service, success is problematical indeed.

The prescription, then, was ignored by politicians: in Britain in a hurry to evade power, and in a hurry in Africa to seize power. But the diagnosis remained correct. What followed, and what may still come to pass, is described in my essay, "Broken-backed States".

The term 'broken-backed government' has been accepted by many English political scientists to describe a certain political condition. The term has—perhaps predictably—found less favour in academic and political circles in the new states. Some Asian and African readers seem not to have noticed that, while emphasising the flimsiness of the apparatus of government, I have also drawn attention to the enduring qualities of the social infrastructure. Elsewhere, I have observed that:

> 'Whereas in Anglo-Saxondom, [politics and political organisation] provide the skeleton and the nervous system of the body national, in Burma they are little more than a cloak. Party organisation is inchoate ... thereby Burma has survived twenty years of near-anarchy without serious strain. The essential core of national life is the cycle of festivals, the myriad pagodas and monasteries, the community of the market-place and the rice-field. All this has maintained the thread of continuity: and Burma has survived.'[13]

Probably the most fruitful development in Asian political studies of

[13] "The Politics of Burma" in Saul Rose (ed.), *Politics in Southern Asia*, London and New York, 1963, p. 115.

recent years has been the coming together of anthropologists and political scientists. The anthropologists have begun to study the political process as offering a specially eloquent illustration of the operation of social relations and 'networks'. Students of politics have examined the different relationships between, and inside, rural communities, tribes, castes, and other groups in order to understand the actual power-nexus of politics. One of my earliest efforts to think in sociological terms about political history was a paper originally contributed to a conference held at the Royal Anthropological Institute in connection with the centenary of the birth of Charles Darwin: "Race, Nationalism and Communalism in Asia".

The Asian leader who most profoundly regarded politics and political institutions as aspects of social change, social service, and individual self-development was Gandhi. As indicated earlier, my own academic appraisals, stemming from my own individual experience, have concentrated upon how people actually operate the machinery of government: I have been attracted neither by formal, constitutional, legalistic studies, nor by the theory and the philosophy of politics. Yet somehow the magnetism of Gandhi, and of other original Indian thinkers has drawn me into a reconsideration of the fundamentals of politics, the universal questions, which a contemporary historian might not ordinarily seek to analyse.

My paper, "Magnificent Failure?—The Gandhian Ideal in India", was written in response to different stimuli. First, it is a tribute to the Indian political renaissance as one of the great contributions (like the French Revolution or the American Revolution) to the emancipation of mankind and the fuller realisation of individual man as a liberated being. Then, it is a protest against the debasement of the message of a great man by lesser men, who seek to exploit the true word for baser purposes. And thirdly it is an appeal to thinking men in the West to hearken to the inner voice of Asia.

Earlier, I gave my view that academic students of politics, like lesser beings, are 'down there among the amoebae, wriggling with all the rest'. Whatever I may have written about the advantages of detachment, which an academic niche provides, the past decade has been a time when my connection with southern Asia has been a major influence in shaping my reactions to politics in my own native land. Elsewhere, I have recorded my debt to Asia in shaping my whole intellectual and emotional outlook.[14] Here I attempt to define the role of Asia—mainly of India—in helping to provide me with a coherent political philosophy. It also seems worth suggesting how techniques evolved in analysing Asian politics are relevant to the observation of western politics, when so much of current British psephology and other political methodology is mechanical and superficial. "East and West: Reflections after a General Election October 1964" concludes this collection of essays.

This, then, is what remains of the harvest, 'reaped, or lost'. During this last ten years, I have been compelled to discard many fondly-held beliefs: but out of it all has emerged a reasonably consistent and coherent point of view. As it seems to me, looking around the world, the raw material of politics, the sociological foundation, exhibits every kind of difference. The extent to which the individual is immersed in the community, the nature of the community, the extent to which authority is equipped to control the community, the efficiency of communication between authority and the community: these are only the most generalised outlines of some of the variables which go into the foundations of politics.

Yet the positive operation of politics is essentially undifferentiated: the assertion of will, the active application of man's mind upon circumstances. The fundamentals of political debate, such as the reconciliation of authority and the community with the claim to individual freedom, or the alternatives of compromise and confrontation, recur in all ages and places. A study of the sociology of Asian politics is likely to emphasise particular characteristics in the Asian environment. A study of the political philosophy of Asia is likely to deal in the universals of politics, even though the concepts employed are of Asian origin. The intermediate ground of political thought in action—the functioning of politics and government— may be expected to mirror sometimes the particular aspects of society and custom, sometimes the universal aspects of political theory. What remains difficult for the western observer is to distinguish between universals and merely Europe-centric concepts. A reviewer of my book, *Ballot Box and Bayonet* (an attempt to assess modern Asian politics without too great an emphasis on European value judgements), writes of my effort 'to redefine democracy in the light

[14] "The Uniqueness of Asia, as seen by a European" in Raghavan Iyer (ed.), *The Glass Curtain*, Oxford, 1965.

of all the justified qualifications of that term in the context of emerging countries'. The reviewer then quotes a conditional clause which I insert: 'Unless democracy is to be drained of all meaning it ought, surely, to include among its fundamentals the right of free speech and free association, together with freedom from arbitrary arrest and the right of fair and open trial.' To all this, the reviewer asks: 'Why?'[15] He regards my *caveat* as evidence of 'the limitations of the western concept of parliamentary democracy'. I still insist that I have stripped away the western accretions and have included only such fundamentals as would be acceptable to non-westerners such as Gandhi or Albert Luthuli. If my reviewer were then to observe that my fundamentals were not acceptable to Sukarno or Nkrumah, I would retort that by now we had discarded 'democracy' for 'guided democracy' or 'Afro-Asian democracy', or some such hybrid.

Let me not claim too much. Remembering Collingwood's dictum that even the great are men of their age, let me be content to remain a minor former imperialist, trying to discover his way through the post-imperial epilogue. I am reminded of the sign which stood by the side of the old road which led from the foothills of Assam by way of Manipur to the Burma border: 'British India ends here. Travellers proceeding beyond this point do so at their own risk.' So it is with the contemporary historian of southern Asia: going beyond British India, one proceeds at one's own risk.

Then let us remember the question of the Master of the Caravan, about to leave on the journey to Samarkand, and the reply:

> *But who are ye in rags and rotten shoes,*
> *You dirty-bearded, blocking up the way?*

> *We are the Pilgrims, master; we shall go*
> *Always a little further; it may be*
> *Beyond that last blue mountain barred with snow,*
> *Across that angry or that glimmering sea . . .*

[15] *New Society*, August 6, 1964: Review: "Asian Politics for Everybody".

I

History in a Time of Transition

HISTORICAL writing, like much else in Asia, is at present passing through a fluid, transitional phase. For nearly 200 years,
historians of Asia have been involved in the great debate that
has revolved around colonialism, both in the sense of economic
exploitation and of imposed government by the West. This debate,
which attained its climax during the half-century 1900–50, has now
been concluded for all practical purposes, the colonial power having
departed, except for a few footholds where—as in Hongkong—withdrawal is only a matter of a few years. But although the debate has
ceased to have any practical significance, the historians of today—
both Asian and western—are still almost entirely absorbed in the
problems which occupied the attentions of their predecessors.

How was it that men who came to Asia as traders stayed to
become administrators? Was their purpose only the economic exploitation of underdeveloped countries, or were they also moved by
higher motives?

These ulterior motives—a desire to spread the light of
Christianity, to introduce a concept of law that was absolute and
nationwide, to create the liberal institutions of responsible government—how far were they dominant? How far successful? What
was the Asian response?

These were some of the questions pondered by western historians. Many of them approached their subject in a mood of fulfilment, seeking to place on record their sense of high achievement;
others wrote in a spirit of inquiry, of doubt and of warning; others

reacted against the whole process of alien domination and exploitation.

On the Asian side, the same topics were the subject of study but (somewhat naturally) often in different terms. Among Asians of the nineteenth century there were thinkers who adopted a western point of view, and who treated the process of alien domination as a necessary stage in the reform and reconstruction of their society: but, as a spirit of revolt against the assumed superiority of the West spread throughout Asia, a different attitude took shape. In general, Asian historians became concerned to re-establish their own civilisations as equal or superior in value to those of the West; they examined colonial activities in Asia to prove that these had damaged and destroyed the pre-existing cultures; and they established 'legends' or 'folk myths' of national struggles against the alien invader.

In short, whereas western writers were largely concerned to justify and explain European intervention in Asia, the Asians were largely concerned to rehabilitate their national esteem and to contribute towards the task of shaking off alien rule: on neither side was it possible to be independent, to stand aloof from the struggle. However scholarly and detached individuals on either side might be, they could not approach history in Asia without becoming subject to all manner of preconceptions and presuppositions. All history was, to some extent, polemic.

The process whereby in the 1940s and '50s complete independence has been attained by most of the nations of South and South-East Asia might have been expected to liberate historians from these preconsiderations. But even when, as in the case of Britain and her former dominions, the transfer of power was made amicably and without the interposition of force, 'colonialism' has left a deep scar upon the minds of both sides of the former relationship.

On the British side, feelings are composed of a curious mixture of guilt and of shaken pride. Colonialism is no longer respectable; the qualities of character, the commercial 'know how' and technical inventiveness, which made it possible for Europeans—more especially the British—to rule, and reap the natural wealth of Asia, are not now in fashion. The self-confidence and sense of mission of the nineteenth-century Briton now has an embarrassing, old-fashioned look.

Yet the British today regard with frustration a world where the Royal Navy is no longer supreme, and where the City of London is no longer the universal banker. Surely things were much better when Britain held dominion over palm and pine? Surely the British Empire cannot just be dismissed by a Marxist sneer?

And so the main themes in British historical writing about Asia in the post-imperial present are still concerned with the impact of colonialism on eastern peoples, and the writers themselves are still mentally and emotionally involved in the process. The 'non-professional' historians, who are mainly former administrators or soldiers, or connected with commerce, write in a valedictory strain, sounding a last reveille for British achievements. The university historians tend to protest their disassociation from imperialism, to condemn the men of the nineteenth century for not foreseeing the course of events in the twentieth century. Revised editions of the standard histories are made, in which the older criticisms of ancient Asian rulers are omitted. But the university historians are just as much obsessed with the colonial régime as other writers personally identified with the old order; they are still taking part in the colonial debate; very few have moved on to a new view of Asian history.

The scholars of other European nations are still involved, perhaps to a greater degree than the British, with the attitude of yesterday. The growing body of American students of Asia are also not wholly *dégagé*: up to very recently, American studies of South and South-East Asia have revealed an emotional anti-colonial bias for which the shade of George III is presumably responsible. Today, as Americans enter to an increasing extent into the affairs of Asia, frequently finding themselves labelled 'imperialists', a considerable reappraisal of the colonial theme is taking place.

But after all, the most important development of the present era is the return of the nations of Asia to their former stature in world affairs. What is the effect of this revival upon Asian historians?

The scar made by colonial rule was mentioned. Asians often stress their need to shake off their 'slave mentality', a consciousness of inferior status, of economic backwardness and of intellectual frustration which many aver is the legacy of colonial rule.

Asian historians have therefore concerned themselves with

underlining even more forcibly the negative aspect of European domination. They have enshrined the memory of heroes of the struggle for national liberation in epic biographies (for which the eight-volume biography of Gandhi by D. G. Tendulkar forms the archetype), they have retold the stories of their countries in terms of resistance to foreign domination.

All this represents a rejection of the European view of Asian countries during the colonial period: but it does not represent a new conception of history. The previous versions represented by the Europeans are inverted, turned inside out, but the subject-matter of history remains the same, even if it is looked at from an opposite angle. Probably the most striking example of this genre is the well-known study of the Indian Mutiny by V. D. Savarkar entitled *The Indian War of Independence*. Savarkar seeks to present an entirely fresh picture of the events of 1857: but practically all his material is drawn from the accounts of British soldiers and British officials of the Mutiny days, and his technique is merely to call their white black. His account revolves round the same old issues: there is no really new interpretation to compare with the genuinely novel interpretation which Mathiez achieved for the French Revolution and Charles A. Beard applied to the American Revolution by re-examining the subject in terms of economic causes.[1]

Savarkar is avowedly a propagandist and is not representative of the more detached scholars of his country. Nevertheless, it is broadly true that the present generation of Asian historians bring to their work technical equipment identical with their western colleagues, they consider similar problems, examine similar evidence— and in almost every case, draw conclusions that are subtly or tremendously different from those of the West. In the view of this writer, there is a danger here: the two sides so often appear to be talking the same language, to be undergoing the same cerebrations, when in reality they are moving in opposite directions.

The Asian, almost inevitably, will see his subject against a background of renascent nationalism: the European cannot adopt this framework for himself, even if he wishes so to do. But to most European scholars, nationalist history is associated with the aberra-

[1] Cf. A. Mathiez, *The French Revolution*, London, 1928, and C. A. Beard, *An Economic Interpretation of the Constitution of the United States*, New York, 1913.

tions of French and German national apologists of the nineteenth century, and the theme has a somewhat hollow ring.

If Asian thinkers are being carried on a wave of nationalism, Europeans still look at the world through European blinkers. The term 'Europe-centric' has been devised to characterise this point of view in which activities in Asia and Africa are considered to be important mainly as they affect Europeans and are motivated by them. It is typical of this attitude that, when in 1946 the University of Cambridge first agreed to include the history of Africa, South America and Asia within the scope of undergraduate studies, the course received the name of "The Expansion of Europe"!

And so it is vitally necessary for historians of East and West to recognise honestly their different viewpoints and agree, frankly, to differ when they must, rather than to snipe at each other from their separate vantage-points. Probably the most important function of the Conference on Asian History held in London in July 1956 was to bring together a gathering of scholars from three continents, giving them the opportunity to talk at length and to discover their variously-held points of view.

2

The City in Asia

BECAUSE of the modern tendency to assess all political institutions in relation to the nation-state, the role of the city has been
neglected in modern political studies. Yet, to the classical Greek
writers, politics, πολιτικα, also meant 'the affairs of cities'. To Plato,
the political community, the republic, is in essence the city. And in
forming this community Plato acknowledges the need for divine
guidance: 'In founding our city, if we are wise, we shall take no
guidance save from our national guide [the Delphian Apollo]. For
surely this god as he gives his guidance from his seat on the
Omphalos in the centre of the earth is the national guide of all
men.'[1] And so, Plato's city derives its legitimacy, its ethos, its fortune from the godhead dwelling on the sacred mountain in the
centre of the earth. Athens, with its Acropolis, symbolises on a
reduced scale the sacred mountain, home of the gods, with the world
of men around. The city mirrors the world.

There was a distinction between what we may call sacred and
profane cities.[2] Some places are natural centres for men to come
together: as trading marts, staging posts, or in proximity to valued
natural resources, they exercised an economic or geographical pull-
ing power. For the sacred city, we can only postulate a supernatural

[1] *The Republic of Plato*, tr. by A. D. Lindsay, London, 1908, Book
IV.

[2] Some of the reflections which follow were suggested by Charles
Carrington.

explanation. What of Rome, which has no natural, strategic, commercial or geographic significance? On the road to nowhere, amid
the rise and fall of temporal dominion, Rome remains the capital of
the western world. Rome: the city of Romulus, the god-king who
was the incarnation of Jupiter. Rome: the city of Peter's martyrdom;
ubi Petrus ibi ecclesia. And so, the road network which connected
the provinces with Imperial Rome still drew men to the eternal city
long after Rome's universal power had crumbled.

The record of the Barbarian kingdoms after the fall of Rome
largely hinges upon the efforts of their rulers to escape from ancient
tribal myths about old, sacred cities by incorporating these into new,
national myths based on the mystique of the monarchy. All the time
there is the ghost of Rome haunting the scene; and the pull of
the sacred city repeatedly upsets the balance of forces. However, the
western kingdoms create their own sacred and royal cities, the
foundation of the national monarchy: Aachen, Rheims, Uppsala,
Tara, Scone. These places do not thereby become commercial capitals. This is a separate, even an opposed development.

Rome also bequeathed to western Europe the political concept
of citizenship and the civic tradition of municipal amenity and
public service. This tradition reappeared in the great trading cities
which arose in the twelfth and thirteenth centuries. In the Europe
of the middle ages, these towns were nurseries of an urban, bourgeois political culture which was to rival and challenge the feudal
pyramid of the countryside: knights, lords, and king. Britain was
not in the mainstream of this urbanisation. When Paris, Naples,
Venice, Milan and Lisbon boasted populations of 100,000 each,
London's total was about 40,000: the same as that of Bruges, and
smaller than Ghent with 50,000 people.

The great municipal tradition only crossed the English Channel
in mutilated form. The British like to think that they possess a
unique genius for local government: but this is quite distinct from
the civic spirit. Probably because English cities were not immured
behind defensive walls, like those in the Low Countries or north
Italy, there has never been a clear distinction between city and
countryside. Since before Shakespeare, the main endeavour of the
successful bourgeois has been to turn himself into a country gentle-
man. The City of London has never dominated England's political
fortunes as Paris has decided those of France. Even today, when the

megalopolis in south-east England is distorting the whole social and economic development of Great Britain, there seems little serious consideration of the role of London in national life. The American political outlook is also shaped much more by the small town, the county, and the state, rather than by the urban, civic tradition. Perhaps it is an example of that ethnocentricity in political thinking which was touched upon earlier that, in their approach to Asia, few Anglo-American historians or students of politics have singled out the city, the capital, for special treatment. Yet Rome, Byzantium, and Jerusalem form part of our common intellectual inheritance.

The sacred city of South and East Asia is the supreme symbol of the state within the unifying cosmology which links together earth and heaven. The universe has been conceived as having a certain form, which is reproduced in the world of men. It is the function of the capital, which represents the state and the world, to symbolise this parallelism. The origins of this system are usually assigned to Sumeria, and the Ziggurat or Mountain of God which was erected by successive Sumerian rulers. These Ziggurats were temples, with successive levels or terraces which were artificial reproductions of the planes of the universe. The system spread to north-western India, to the Chou and Han kingdoms, and to South-East Asia, where it survives into the present day. According to Brahmanic and Buddhist doctrine a magical mountain, Mount Meru, forms the axis of the universe. Its summit is the abode of the supreme war-god, Indra. The two religions differ in the details of their cosmology, but both agree in conceiving of a circular universe; of a focal Mount Meru, home of the gods; of lower continents where spirits and men abide; and of encircling oceans. For a thousand years or more, the capital cities of eastern Asia were designed to reproduce the symbolism of this Brahmanic and Buddhist universe. Sriksetra, the first capital of Burma, was founded according to the chronicles by Indra. In the centre of the city was the palace, *Nan-daw-gon*, upraised, like Mount Meru. The city was surrounded by a circular wall and moat. There were thirty-two gates; an astrological number which corresponded with the thirty-two provinces or vassal states of the kingdom. The thirty-two rulers of these territories, with the king as their head, corresponded with the thirty-three gods who reside on the summit of Meru, with Indra as their chief.

The sacred city was the centre of an agrarian civilisation. The location of the capital was determined mainly in relation to an area of cultivation: very often, an irrigated area. The site of the most famous of the South-East Asian capitals, Angkor, was adjacent both to a fertile agricultural area and to a lake well stocked with fish. The last of the Khmer capitals, Angkor Thom (derived from *Nagara Dham*, the 'great capital'), was built by Jayavarman VII, and like most cosmomagical capitals was rectangular, its sides being directed to the four cardinal points. The central 'mountain' was not a palace, but a Buddhist temple crowned by pinnacles representing, in repetition, the head of Bodhisatva Lokesvara, 'Lord of the World'. The walls were pierced by four gates, with a fifth leading to the entrance to the royal palace. The towers above the gates were also crowned with multiple heads of Lokesvara.

The symbolism of the capital was heightened in China by the device of the inner and inmost city. Historic Peking was primarily separated into two portions, the outer city, known as the Chinese City, and the inner or Tartar City, both being enclosed by walls. Within the Tartar City was the Imperial City, the administrative centre of the empire, and within the Imperial City, the Forbidden City, the abode of the emperor. Access to the Forbidden City was obtained through four gates representing the four cardinal points, of which the southern gate was the most magnificent. Through this gate passed the emperor, and its name, the 'Noon Gate', reflected his noonday-sun splendour. In the very centre of the Forbidden City stood the Throne Hall of Supreme Harmony where the emperor, seated in silence, received the obeisance of his subjects and vassals.

The Forbidden City was laid out in its present form by the Ming emperor Ch'eng Tsu at the beginning of the fifteenth century. The last capital of Burma to be built by a Burmese king, Mandalay, was erected in 1856–7. Yet although Mandalay belongs to the age of the Industrial Revolution, and corrugated-iron roofing forms an important (and effective) element in its architecture, its spirit is that of the immemorial sacred city. Its moated walls were pierced by twelve gates, three each side, inscribed with the signs of the zodiac. The square, moated city was the administrative capital; outside its walls were the commercial and manufacturing suburbs. The moated city contained, within, another royal city, within which were the palaces of the royal family. At the centre was the *Mye-nan-daw* or

'Royal Earth Palace', known to Europeans as the 'Centre of the Universe'. Here was the audience hall where, seated on the Lion Throne, the king faced towards the eastern hills. To the Burmese, the east was the most auspicious direction, and among the royal titles was that of 'Lord of the Sunrise'. The eastern entrance was that through which the king passed.

Having identified some of the topographical symbolism of the sacred city, let us attempt to make an assessment of its political qualities. Because the city represented the state, possession of the capital was the key to rule. After coronation, the kings of Burma, Siam, and Cambodia formally took possession of the realm by going in procession round the walls of the capital: in the case of the Burmese kings, proceeding in the state barge with its lion prow. When this encirclement was completed, the ruler had established his claim to be lord of the universe. Loss of the capital meant, virtually, the ruler's collapse. Because the palace and the city were the emblems of divine rule, their loss meant that the ruler had forfeited his claim to govern. Therefore, palace and city were most carefully guarded. The élite corps of the royal Burmese army, the Guards, was composed of six inner and six outer guard regiments. The six inner regiments guarded the palace and its approaches; the outer regiments guarded the city gates and took their regimental titles from these gates. Should a pretender succeed in gaining possession of the palace, then the whole apparatus of government, almost automatically, passed into his hands. Kings who felt insecure would remain within the palace, fearful to venture forth into their realm in case they might forfeit their claim to rule. Then the citadel would become the prison; and by their self-immurement, rulers many times contributed to their own downfall. Mindon Min, the penultimate king of Burma, came to power by gaining hold of the capital during the absence of his brother, the reigning monarch. Twelve years later, an attempt to seize the palace by *coup de main* was only narrowly thwarted. Thereafter, Mindon never left his capital. His successor, Thibaw Min, felt so insecure that he did not even dare to leave his palace for the city-encircling ceremonial. Surrounded by a sycophantic court, he utterly miscalculated the balance of power in the unknown world outside, and rapidly brought on his own downfall.

Because the city represented the state, the luck or prosperity of the ruler and the country inhered in the city. The foundation of a new city could bring about an acquisition of fortune. National and international fortune or misfortune would be interpreted as deriving from the luck of the capital. If this was clearly exhausted, then the city must be abandoned and a new capital established. This concept of auspiciousness is known to the Chinese as *feng-shui*, the influences of wind and water which bring prosperity to cities and temples, and which must be carefully cultivated. In Burma, the *mingala*, the royal auspiciousness of cities, has been a fickle quality. New foundations have been frequent. Under the last dynasty, the *Konbaung* line, there were no less than six changes of capital, and within thirty years of the founding of Mandalay, Thibaw was being urged to shift the capital yet again. Frequently, a new dynasty would establish a new capital and would sometimes take their name from the city of their choice. The present ruling family in Thailand is sometimes known as the Bangkok dynasty, because the founder moved the capital from the ruins of Ayudhya to the new site. Examples of the luck of a city influencing the ruler are not confined to eastern Asia. In India, Ahmad Shah Bahmani, having undergone illness at Gulbarga, decided that the place was unlucky and moved to Bidar; while Akbar, having lost two children at Agra, became convinced that the city was inauspicious and moved the capital to Fathpur Sikri.

The sacred city, centre of an agrarian society, forms the basis for the imperial city: which, for present purposes, may be defined as the administrative and strategic nerve-centre of the empire of conquest in Asia. Peking, an astrological city in its final form, is an imperial city, founded in order to keep guard against the northern invaders of the Middle Kingdom. François Bernier described the Mughal capital, Delhi, as 'a military encampment'.[3] Delhi, like Peking, is well sited to repel a northern invader. But as the direction of the threat shifted, so the capital might be transferred to an entirely different position. Striking examples occurred under the Tughlak dynasty of Delhi. Tughlakabad, the third of the ruined cities of Delhi, was founded in 1321. Later, Muhammad Tughlak, confronted with revolt in the Deccan, decided to transfer the capital to Deogarh in central India, which he renamed Daulatabad. The in-

[3] F. Bernier, *Travels in the Mogul Empire*, London, 1891, p. 104.

habitants of Delhi were compelled to leave their homes for the new capital. The rebellion of the viceroy of Multan brought the sultan back to the north; and his capital returned to Delhi. But again, in 1340, he went back to Daulatabad, once more taking the Delhi population along with him. After the death of Muhammad, a new capital, Firozabad, was built at Delhi only a few miles from the gaunt walls of deserted Tughlakabad.

The factors which controlled the life of the medieval Asian city still count in an interpretation of the politics of the present day.

The symbolism of the capital has continued to exercise a special influence in China since the 1911 revolution. Sun Yat-sen's party deliberately exploited Nanking, the old southern capital of the Mings, as their rallying-point in order to emphasise the native, Chinese character of their movement in opposition to the Ch'ing emperor, descended from foreign invaders, at the northern capital. When the last child-emperor was caused to abdicate in 1912, he was permitted to retain the imperial title and to occupy the Forbidden City: and so, in the eyes of many conservatives, he remained the Son of Heaven. Only with his ejection from the Forbidden City in 1924 did schemes for his restoration finally collapse. Meanwhile, the struggle between Sun's Kuomintang and the northern leaders revolved, to a degree, around the claims of the northern and southern capitals. In 1928, the Kuomintang captured Peking, confirming the primacy of the national capital at Nanking. Peking was renamed Peiping, or Northern Peace. The symbolism of the new China, united under the Kuomintang, was soon challenged by the Japanese invader. An attempt to secure legitimacy for a Japanese-sponsored régime was made by installing a puppet government in Nanking. The capture of Peking by the communists, and its restoration as the national capital, is resisted by the Kuomintang and many of their American supporters in the only way open to them: by obstinately continuing to refer to Peking as Peiping.

Another country where the character of the revolution was symbolised by a change of capital was Turkey, with the transfer of authority from Levantine Istanbul to Anatolian Ankara. In the 1940s, Marshal Phibun Songkram planned to move the capital of Thailand from Bangkok (linked with the reigning Çakkri dynasty) to the site of a former capital in Lopburi, as a means of enhancing his own prestige. His plan was thwarted by his fall from power in 1945. The key importance of the capital, Bangkok, has been apparent in each of the successive *coups* from 1932 to 1958. On every occasion, when an army has demonstrated its control over the capital, the former ruler has accepted the *fait accompli*, even though he might still be able to command reserves of power. Thus, when Marshal Sarit's troops occupied Bangkok, Marshal Phibun quietly fled the country. Recent events in South Vietnam take on a deeper significance if related to palace and capital. When the old imperial palace at Hué was set alight, conservative Vietnamese deduced that the dynasty of Gia Long had exhausted its mandate, and support was withdrawn from the emperor, Bao Dai. His successor, President Ngo Dinh Diem, attempted to assume many of the trappings of monarchy. Yet he became increasingly isolated from the people, living a withdrawn life within the presidential palace, somewhat reminiscent of the last days of Thibaw at Mandalay. The final attack upon the palace, and the sudden downfall of the régime, exactly reproduced the traditional pattern.

The latest attempt to change the 'luck' of the state by the foundation of a new city has occurred in Pakistan, where the capital has been transferred from Karachi, associated with the corruption of the old party politicians, to Islamabad, an entirely new creation in the foothills of the Himalaya. Here, President Ayub Khan hopes to build the visual symbols of a modern, progressive polity.

Perhaps the most dramatic example of the planned capital, symbol of a nation in making, is New Delhi (not forgetting Washington, DC). Originally called into being as a deliberate political gesture, New Delhi is a fascinating study in political-architectural symbolism. As an imperial power, Britain has left only the most meagre architectural memorials; yet in New Delhi the British created, in Clemenceau's mordant phrase, what is likely to be the most magnificent of all the ruins.

Although the principal architects, Sir Edwin Lutyens and Sir Herbert Baker, may not have acquired a profound knowledge of Asian cosmology, they certainly did insist upon the symbolism of a central hill feature as the *clou* in their overall design. Originally, New Delhi was to stand upon the Ridge: then, because the Ridge area offered inadequate space, officials proposed a level site with no distinguishing eminence. Baker insisted that the principal government buildings should form an acropolis; he quoted from St Matthew, 'A city that is set on an hill cannot be hid.' The two architects visited a number of ancient Indian cities and then, in their *Planning Report* submitted in March 1913, declared: 'The old buildings that have most impressed the imagination of mankind are those raised upon an eminence, such as those of ancient Greek cities and the Capitol at Rome.'[4] Their arguments were accepted, and Raisina Hill became the nucleus of their plans, imparting to them an unrivalled dramatic effect. The Kingsway or Rajpath forms the main approach to the acropolis. The vista of Kingsway evokes in its composition all the attributes of the British Indian Empire. First, there is the statue of the king-emperor; then the colossal memorial to the Indian Army, one of the two pillars of the British Raj. The other pillar, the Civil Service, receives lapidary recognition in the Secretariat, whose two wings dominate Raisina Hill, with the Viceroy's House behind. The circular building of the central legislature has no place in this composition, and stands somewhat detached: a not inaccurate architectural judgement on the relative importance of parliamentarians and administrators, before, and even after, independence. It may not be too fanciful to suggest that the famous quarrel between Lutyens and Baker possessed symbolic overtones. Lutyens had supposed that a gently sloping ramp between the two wings of the Secretariat would serve to reveal the great Viceroy's House (larger than Versailles) as the crowning feature of the hill complex. By giving the ramp a steep incline, Baker (intentionally or not) succeeded in masking the Viceroy's House so that only its dome is visible from Kingsway, while the pillared Secretariat stands out supreme. Lutyens broke off the collaboration, convinced that Baker was jealous of his masterpiece.[5] Yet who, studying the role of the president in the Indian political system, would not be inclined to acknowledge that Baker's architectural insight has been confirmed by events?

From the imperial city let us turn to the market city, the international bazaar, which has been of peculiar importance in Asia. The state based upon maritime and commercial power evolves on very different lines from the agrarian state. This development cannot be studied better than in South-East Asia, in the oceanic empires

[4] C. Hussey, *Life of Sir Edwin Lutyens*, London, 1950, pp. 286–7.
[5] Lutyens later observed: 'Here I met my Bakerloo.'

of Srivijaya and its successors. Let us examine, in a little more detail, the emergence of Malacca and Acheh.

If you have read the description of Tomé Pires: 'Malacca is a city that was made for merchandise, fitter than any in the World', you will expect great things.[6] Yet, as one stands by the sluggish, meandering creek of today, with sufficient draught for little more than a barge, it is difficult to conjure up a picture of the city concerning which legend says that 'A cat took a whole year to cover all the tiles'. One must begin by discarding present-day impressions of a great port: as van Leur reminds us, our 'more presumptuous modern terminology' needs to be adjusted to the scale of past centuries.[7] The significance of the port city of yesterday is not to be measured by the dimensions of today. Malacca in its heyday during the fifteenth century was the meeting-place of the Near and Far East. Unlike the agrarian empires, the market city's importance had nothing to do with access to a granary (Malacca always depended upon food imports from overseas). It rested upon its maritime importance in relation to the monsoons, the currents in the Straits, and the absence of other natural anchorages on the west coast of Malaya. The other great market cities of South-East Asia, such as Acheh, and later Singapore, similarly owed their importance to their position upon the trade routes: they became empires not of the land but of the ocean.

To acquire parity of esteem, the rulers of Malacca invested themselves with the trappings of the sacred city. The *kraton* or palace was placed upon the peak now known as St Paul's Hill, and the aristocratic official hierarchy was marshalled in numbers with astrological significance (4, 8, 16, 32) on the correct cosmological pattern. But the greatness of Malacca derived from its trade and its foreign trading community. The foremost group were merchants from Gujarat, with others from Bengal, Coromandel, Arabia, and Indonesia. Tomé Pires asserts that eighty-four languages were spoken in Malacca. In order to regulate foreign trade, to levy the customs dues on which the revenues depended, and to control the foreigners, four *shahbandars* or port superintendents were appoin-

[6] A. Cortesão, *The Suma Oriental of Tomé Pires*..., London, 1944, Vol. II, Book 6.

[7] J. C. van Leur, *Indonesian Trade and Society*, The Hague, 1955, p. 403.

ted. One *shahbandar* dealt exclusively with the Gujaratis; one with the merchants from Bengal, Pegu, and Pasai; one with the various Indonesians; and a fourth with the traders of Indo-China and China. The foreigners had their own sections in the town and their own spokesmen or captains. There were special courts to try cases involving the foreigners. Whereas the sacred and imperial city was introverted and static, cherishing its protocol from age to age, the market city was outward-looking, assimilating beliefs and techniques from the culturally dominant East or West: pioneering, for example, the spread of Islam. Though these new influences leapt from one port town to the next, penetration into the interior was much more slow. Like lighthouses, the port towns glittered with their cosmopolitan commerce; but little of this effulgence seeped into the fishing villages and the paddy lands of the *ra'ayats*.

The plural society, usually associated with the European colonial era, was well established in the pre-colonial period. Indeed, it was the familiarity of the port towns with foreign merchants which made their rulers and *shahbandars* so ready to accept the Europeans. When Malacca fell to the Portuguese, much of its trade passed to Acheh. Again, merchants gathered from every corner of Asia—from Turkey, the Levant, Arabia, Malabar, Coromandel, Bengal, Arakan, and Pegu, with the Gujaratis again dominant. The foreigners resided in their own *kampongs* and were subject to special mixed courts, presided over by the *laxamana* or governor of Acheh. The prosperity of trade rested upon the understanding reached between the Gujaratis and the Achinese nobility, the *orangkaya*.

The cosmopolitan merchants who built up these market cities—Gujaratis, Armenians, Parsees, and others—also provided the essential nucleus for the great western port cities in Asia. From the Asian prototype emerged yet another kind of city, well described by K. M. Panikkar in *Asia and Western Dominance*. He writes (p. 501):

The new cities which grew up as a result of European contacts, Bombay, Calcutta, and Madras, Shanghai, Tientsin, Singapore, Colombo, Jakarta, etc., represent a new principle: the organisation of the city as an independent unit. In Madras, Calcutta and Bombay we have the full paraphernalia of European city life, with sheriffs, mayors, corporations and aldermen. From this point of view, the organisation of the Municipal Committee of Shanghai by the British merchants, and its phenomenal growth during a period of seventy years, may represent a greater and more far-reaching change than the control exercised by the foreigners on the imperial court. . . . It is the city that has created the wealthy middle classes in India, China and other Asian countries. . . . The possibility of the great cities surviving as centres of civilisation, even if regression sets in elsewhere inside the countries of Asia much in the same way as in medieval Europe, cannot be overlooked, and if that happens the credit for the survival of the new life in the great cities will certainly belong to Europe.

As Sardar Panikkar points out, the new cities were distinguished from their predecessors by two main features: the merchants, from being the coadjutors of the noble officials in city government, now emerged themselves as governors; while the immense growth in population of the new cities turned them into an entirely different urban phenomenon. Writing only ten years ago, Panikkar did not foresee that the second feature, the rise of a mass proletariat, would very soon overwhelm the first, the dominance of the mercantile class.

The character of these new cities was commercial and cosmopolitan. Wherever business looked promising, the international business houses would extend their agencies. A typical example is that of the Sassoon family. David Sassoon landed in Bombay in 1832, having originally come from Baghdad. With his long Arab gown and patriarchal beard he was soon a familiar yet elusive figure in Bombay. A shrewd financier and a great philanthropist he endowed the city with many of its public institutions. When the foreign settlement of Shanghai was established, Sassoon was among the first to open a branch, in 1845. His son, Elias David Sassoon, merchant and banker, pioneered the development of the Bombay cotton industry, and continued the endowment of schools, hospitals, and libraries. A later Sassoon, Sir Victor (1882–1961), transferred most of the family assets to Shanghai after the first world war, investing heavily in industry and in real estate, including the celebrated Cathay Hotel. This type of financier regarded nationality as offering little more than the protection of a passport: but he did entertain feelings of obligation and responsibility towards the cities where his fortune had been made.

Because of the cosmopolitan character of the business community, almost all the great port cities were partially or even totally divorced from the cultural milieu of their hinterland. What had the atmosphere of Rangoon in its trading heyday to do with Burma? Or Singapore with inland Malaya? Or even Bombay and Calcutta with India? Very little, it seems. Kipling, with his habitual flair, sensed the difference when he wrote in *City of Dreadful Night* (ch. 1): 'We are all backwoodsmen and barbarians together—we others dwelling beyond the Ditch in the outer darkness of the Mofussil. . . . We have left India behind us at Howrah Station, and now we enter foreign parts.' During the nineteenth century, despite the western impact, rural society went on very much as before, whereas the port cities were already experiencing the transforming influence of political, educational, social and economic westernisation.

The origins of the modern political system in India may, without too much extravagance, be traced back to the granting of a charter in 1687 for the establishment of a municipal corporation in Madras, followed in 1726 by similar charters for Bombay and Calcutta. These municipal bodies were closed corporations, insulated from popular pressure, and contributing little to civic life. Yet, from early in the nineteenth century, a demand for means of political expression began to stir, especially in Calcutta. Calcutta supported a small but vigorous periodical press: *The Calcutta Journal*, *The Friend of India*, and *Hurkaru* in English, together with *Sambad Kaumudi*, *Sambad Chandrika*, and *Timir Nausak* in Bengali. Attempts to impose restrictions under the Press Act aroused the ire of merchants and lawyers and the campaign led to the Free Press Dinner and a public petition, organised by Dwarkanath Tagore and T. Dickens on the lines of contemporary English popular agitation. During the 1860s and 1870s, both in Calcutta and Bombay, a strong demand developed for greater popular control over municipal affairs, which led to the introduction of Bills to reform both corporations (Bombay 1872, Calcutta 1876). Leaders such as Pherozeshah Mehta in Bombay and Kristo Das Pal in Calcutta, products of the new institutions of learning—lawyers, newspaper editors, and other professional men—now began to exercise great influence, along with reforming Englishmen, like the merchant George Yule.

When the Indian National Congress was formed, almost all its front-rank leadership was recruited from the municipal corporations of the Presidency capitals, to the exclusion of the rest of India. These men alone had acquired experience of public debate, they had formed some kind of philosophy of political action, and through encounters with senior British officials they had learned something of the art of dealing with the bureaucracy. As late as 1905, Lord Curzon declared to the secretary of state (in a dispatch dated February 2): 'Calcutta is the centre from which the Congress party is manipulated throughout the whole of Bengal and indeed the whole of India.'

Asians were not able to play the same leading role in city government, outside India and Ceylon. In Rangoon and Singapore, the European mercantile community dominated civic affairs. Even so, the example of non-officials challenging the *ipse dixit* of the officials was not without its effect, while even as a minority in the councils, Asians could learn from experience. There were other side-effects: when the first Rangoon municipal elections were held in June 1882, a number of Burmese ladies came forward as voters and canvassers: probably the earliest Asian example of the exercise of female suffrage.

Perhaps the most remarkable of these examples of city government was the Shanghai Municipality. Three British merchants were invited to form a Committee of Roads and Jetties in 1845, and nine years later the municipal council proper was founded, consisting of five members elected by a public meeting. The council was responsible to the fourteen consuls representing foreign powers with extra-territorial rights and to an annual meeting of ratepayers. In 1863, the concession became the International Settlement. Gradually, British control gave way to a wider representation: by 1930, the municipal council comprised five British, five American, two Japanese, and five Chinese members; and the annual meeting of ratepayers had become so large that it had to be held on the race-course. Shanghai provided a city of refuge for the reformers, during the last decades of the Ch'ing dynasty. As early as 1864, newspapers were appearing in English and Chinese. After the Boxer rising, revolutionary articles began to be published in Shanghai, and the International Settlement provided a base for the supporters of Sun Yat-sen; Sun himself lived in Shanghai after the collapse of his first republican venture. The powerful Soong family which played such an influential role in the Kuomintang period derived their fortune largely from the city of Shanghai.

The political experiment of municipal self-government hinged upon the rise of a professional, mercantile middle class: this class was the main pivot for the expansion of western higher education. The first western teaching institutions in Asia were the Catholic missionary colleges of Goa and Manila, but these were designed to sustain the faith rather than to spread western learning. The earliest of the new model western colleges were founded in Calcutta: not on the initiative of the British government, but in response to, and largely following the initiative of the Hindu commercial and professional classes. The Hindu College (later Presidency College) was established in 1817 by the efforts of David Hare, a rationalist watchmaker, and Ram Mohan Ray, a philosophical Brahman official. Among the benefactors were Dwarkanath Tagore, banker and industrialist, and several of the Tagores were among the first pupils. Christian missionary societies established other colleges in Calcutta and its suburbs, and within two decades thousands of Calcutta youths were receiving a higher education through the medium of English. Because the goal of the *novus homo*, the western-educated Indian, was government service, this provides a rough guide to the lead established by the port cities over the provinces. Let us examine the results of the examinations held for the recruitment of *munsifs*, the judges in the lesser courts, for the Lower Provinces in 1841, as a typical case. Among the successful candidates, three came from Dacca, four from Murshidabad, seven from Patna, and forty from Calcutta. The foundation of universities in the three Presidency cities in 1857 further heightened their intellectual predominance over the rest of India. Students flocked from upcountry to the great cities: indeed, they even came from Ceylon to Madras and from Burma to Calcutta. Despite strenuous efforts after 1920 to decentralise university education and to bring forward new foundations, even today the universities of Calcutta, Bombay, and Madras—together with Delhi—dominate Indian higher education to an extent comparable with Oxford and Cambridge in England.

Other Asian port cities had to wait longer for their western-style universities. The foundation stone of a college at Singapore was laid by Raffles in June 1823: ten years later, a local newspaper described the college as 'an unfinished building or ruin', 'a convenient shelter for thieves': Singapore had to wait another one hundred and twenty years for its university. Similarly, Colebrook's proposal for a university college in Colombo, made in 1833, was not fulfilled until 1921. Nevertheless, in these cities, as in Rangoon and Shanghai, colleges and high schools were founded by missionary endeavour, by mercantile philanthropy, and by municipal or government action. An institution such as the Free School at Penang may seem unimportant by present-day standards, but its influence in the local setting may have been equal to that of many of the universities of the West.

In consequence of the impact of western education, and of contacts with overseas, the port cities evolved a new society, unique in Asia, which was to a large degree liberated (or isolated, according to one's point of view) from the bonds of community and custom. The archetype of the liberated Asian metropolitan man is Henry Derozio, the Eurasian schoolmaster at Hindu College, the Chatterton of Calcutta. Under his influence, young Brahmans refused investiture with the sacred threefold thread and defied the orthodox.

> *And when your torch shall dissipate the gloom,*
> *That long has made your country but a tomb,*
> *Or worse than tomb, the priest's, the tyrant's den,*
> *Guide on, young men: your course is well begun.*

So wrote Derozio: destined himself for an early and unquiet grave. Not all social change has been so furious as with Derozio's young Bengali disciples: but in all the Asian port cities, middle classes have emerged which are set apart from their country cousins. Such, for example, were the 'Queen's Chinese' of Singapore, Malacca, and Penang: an English-educated group whose loyalties and tastes were directed towards England. Such were the Parsees of Bombay and Karachi. Entertaining novel views of marriage and the family and the place of women in society, the cosmopolitans formed a distinct, new caste. Having rejected the limitations of tradition, in order to shake free from the old bonds of family and community, they found themselves, willy-nilly, consigned to a new category in society. Among the many vignettes of Calcutta life depicted by Nirad C. Chaudhuri in *The Autobiography of an Unknown Indian* there is a description of the Anglicised Bengalis (pp. 396–7).

'They lived in aristocratic segregation', he says, 'brought about in the first instance by the orthodoxy of the ordinary Bengali, who considered them to have lost caste, and secondly by their own contempt for those whom they looked upon as the unredeemed. . . . They had made their choice for the West and lived in the light of their convictions.' Chaudhuri talks of this group in the past tense: he does not regard the *déclassé* of today as their equivalent. Nor can we find the successors to the Anglophile Queen's Chinese. Their passing is a symptom of the shift in the balance of forces which has resulted in the upper-class cosmopolitanism of yesterday being replaced by what (for want of a more specific term) we must call the popular nationalism of today. As the merchants gave way to the masses, so the trading city became the industrial city. Although the beginnings of industrialisation occurred in the nineteenth century, the really significant changes have been recent. Beginning, usually, with processing and extractive manufactures, like jute and rice mills, the port cities now include a full range of industrialisation. This has created a demand for a new kind of labour force, large in number, with only rudimentary skills. This urban proletariat now gives the great cities their prevailing character.

As late as 1910, the population of Calcutta and Bombay was in each case under one million. Fifty years later, Calcutta's total almost touched three million; while if Howrah and other suburbs are included, the conurbation now houses over five and a half million souls. Over the same period, the population of greater Bombay exceeded four million. During the same half-century, the total population of Shanghai has risen from one and a half million (1916 census) to an estimated seven million. Rates of growth like these are vastly in excess of those in western cities, and several times higher than the general, overall growth rate in Asian countries. It is in the great metropolitan cities that future population trends are most incalculable: but some surveys already envisage conurbations composed of twenty million persons in India at the end of the century.

Even though the industrial city-dwellers may try to re-create a semblance of the community life of the settled, traditional habitations from which they have come, and congregate in streets and quarters which are inhabited by those of their own tribe and tongue, the great cities are warrens of instability and insecurity. Law and order penetrate not at all into the hidden alleys and courts of the great Asian city. The city-dwellers live always near the flash-point of social and political hysteria. The mass politics of the modern Asian city is the politics of extremism and violence.

When, in the 1920s, nationalism in the form of racialism became the domineering voice in Asia, race-hatred first manifested itself in the great cities: those cities which previously had shown a cosmopolitan tolerance and agreement to differ. In Shanghai and the other Treaty Ports, hatred of the European was prompted by the Left and the Right. In the words of a manifesto issued by the Comintern's Congress of Toilers of the Far East (1922), 'In these quarters foreign bourgeois, fattened on other men's blood and sweat, ride about in carriages drawn by men-horses, the rickshaws, hastening them with kicks and sticks.' The foreigner did not have to be a European. On May 26, 1930, in the centre of Rangoon, from three to five hundred Indians were killed and about one thousand injured by Burmese mobs, enraged because Indian coolies secured employment before Burmese in the Rangoon docks. In India, the gathering clouds of Hindu–Muslim conflict first broke into storm in the congested city centres, as in Cawnpore in March 1931 when two to five thousand persons were killed in two days of rioting. The climax came at the moment of independence when the worst of all the bloodletting occurred in Delhi and Calcutta. The city mob—a political phenomenon largely forgotten in Britain and North America—remains a deadly danger which may at any time be aroused. Lahore, Bombay, Colombo, Singapore, Jakarta: all have been plunged into blind chaos by appeals to race or religion during the last ten years.

The political philosophies which have exercised the widest influence in the Asia of our time, those of Gandhian India and Mao-ist China, have both sought to renounce the city, which both regard as alien to the spirit of their movement, and to rebuild the community through the countryside.

Rabindranath Tagore, with his universal outlook, was able to understand that a balance might be achieved between city and countryside.

Villages [he observes] are nearer to nature than towns, and in closer touch with the fountain of life.... It is the function of the village ... to provide people with their elemental needs, with food and joy, with the simple poetry of life. [But the town provides scope for individuality and competition] and so in the town, where the pressure of the community is relaxed, the individual mind gets a chance to rise superior to the mass mind—'rustic' is everywhere a synonym for the mind's narrowness. [Tagore felt that] when the community does not incline to one side—the village and the town have harmonious interaction, [but between the twentieth-century industrial city and the village, he believed] a gulf is formed and goes on widening. City and village then stand forth as exploiter and victim.... Our modern cities...feed upon the social organism that runs through the villages. They appropriate the life stuff of the villages and slough off a huge amount of dead matter, while making a lurid counterfeit of prosperity.

And so, Tagore abandoned the family mansion in Calcutta; and the remainder of his life was devoted to rural reconstruction at Santiniketan.[8]

The Gandhian ideal also, and even more completely, looked to the village as the source of India's regeneration; and Jayaprakash Narayan in attempting to interpret Gandhi in his *Plea for Reconstruction of Indian Polity* (1959) is least convincing in his proposals for the problems posed by the industrial conurbation. The massive programme of Community Development, which now embraces almost all the Indian countryside, stops short at the town. The Third Five Year Plan frankly admits (p. 290): 'In the plans hitherto formulated urban areas have not been actively associated', and it does little or nothing to fill the gap.

The Chinese communist ideological emphasis upon rural as opposed to urban revolutionary techniques emerged from the grim struggle with the Kuomintang. The first communist group was organised under Comintern auspices in the French Concession at Shanghai in 1922, and began to operate according to the Marxist-Leninist thesis by urban, industrial action. However, the Kuomintang, which at first accepted the communists as partners, decided that they must be eliminated and in the big cities they were captured

[8] See "City and Village", lectures delivered by Tagore at Santiniketan in 1928, included in a commemorative anthology, *Towards Universal Man*, Bombay, 1961.

and exterminated. Away in Hunan, Mao Tse-tung was thinking in terms of rural, peasant support. In a report to the party made in 1927, Mao wrote: 'If we allot ten points to the accomplishment of the democratic revolution, then the urban dwellers and the military rate only three points while the remaining seven points should go to the peasants in their rural revolution.' For some time, this radical departure from orthodoxy was refused recognition. A central committee was reconstituted in Shanghai under Li Li-san, and for some years there were, virtually, rival urban and rural communist movements. The Shanghai headquarters was not finally abandoned until 1933, but meanwhile an entirely new movement had been built up in Kiangsi. Subsequent ideological development with its emphasis upon land reform, the communes, and the Great Leap Forward has served to perpetuate the rural, peasant character of the Chinese Revolution, seen in such formulae as the 'rice bag and bayonet' answer—rural guerrilla war—to the threat of nuclear destruction.

However great the significance of these Asian attempts to evolve constructive alternatives to the urbanisation and suburbanisation of political and social life to which we have succumbed in the West, they must be set alongside the continuing—and, indeed, growing—dominance of the city in Asia. This is noticeable, even in the smaller, less industrialised countries. Of Burma, Thailand, and the Philippines it can be said that the whole of industrial and technical development, of intellectual activity, of political power and administrative control is concentrated within twelve miles of the centre of Rangoon, Bangkok, and Manila. In Thai, *ḳan muang*, which is the usual term for politics, means literally, 'business of the city'. However much political leaders in Asian countries may attempt to call upon the countryside to redress the balance of the town, politics, in theory and in practice, will long continue to be first and foremost the 'business of the city'.

3

Community Development

A NEW PHILOSOPHER'S STONE?

IN the vocabulary of government among the newly-independent nations of Asia and Africa, Community Development is a term of power. Whatever the political system, democratic or autocratic, it is likely to be held in esteem. What is this new Open Sesame? In a United Nations document we read:

Community Development means the process by which the efforts of the people themselves are united with those of governmental authorities to improve the economic, social and cultural conditions of communities, to integrate these communities into the life of the nation and to enable them to contribute fully to national progress. The distinctive features of Community Development programmes are the participation by the people themselves in efforts to improve their level of living with reliance as much as possible on their own initiative: and the provision of technical and other services in ways which encourage initiative, self-help and mutual help and make them more effective.[1]

This definition postulates a situation which has seldom been

[1] *Public Administration Aspects of Community Development Programmes*, ST/TAO/M/14, New York, 1959, p. 2.

49

attained in Asia and Africa. Initiative and self-help, which are invoked above as latent forces waiting to be tapped, have to be laboriously, artificially generated for the service of the village community: this is the prime function of Community Development in the conditions of today.

The Asian villager, whether his economic condition is wretched or tolerable, feels himself a creature of circumstances. Throughout history he has never looked beyond his immediate horizons. He has little sense of belonging to the wider community. He regards authority, especially that of government, as a power to be evaded when possible, or placated when not. The dynamic element in society—the ruling middle class, with its monopoly of western education, political leadership, and economic power—is confined to the town, where there is life, movement, and (for the fortunate few) closer assimilation to the standards of the opulent West. In the countryside there is stagnation and stasis.

Its enthusiasts claim that Community Development provides the nostrum for this malady. They look at the village and diagnose its need for economic improvement, social education, and a sense of participation in the national political process. They argue that the village possesses an untapped asset in its sense of community and solidarity, and they plan to capitalise this asset by associating the village folk in a combined effort towards reconstruction and uplift.

It is often assumed that the introduction of a Community Development scheme conjures new attitudes into life. This paper attempts to examine the actual working of Community Development by means of three studies, taken from South-East Asia. These seek to show the interplay of political and social forces which affect the theoretical application of the principles of Community Development. This does not constitute a criticism of the movement to give a new deal to the Asian villager: far from it. To adapt words used by Sir Malcolm Darling, one of the pioneers in this field, shortcomings and false hopes 'are an argument not for giving up the attempt to re-establish [the village community]—it is far too seriously needed for that—but for fresh experiments, until the appropriate form for each part of [Asia] is discovered'.[2]

[2] *At Freedom's Door*, London, 1950, p. 315.

THE PHILIPPINES

The pattern in the Philippines emerged out of a feverish political tussle and under the aegis of American influence and aid, reflecting the general trend of contemporary Filipino public life. There are two main rivals in the field of development: the organisation controlled by the Presidential Assistant on Community Development (PACD), and the Philippine Rural Reconstruction Movement (PRRM). The precursor of PACD was the National Movement for Free Elections (NAMFREL): this was formed as a reply to the fraud and violence of the 1949 presidential elections. As secretary for defence, Ramon Magsaysay was foremost in safeguarding fair and free conditions for the 1951 elections, and NAMFREL moved its resources behind him and his decision to run for president. The National Movement for Free Elections sponsored the opening of rural community centres as 'workshops of democracy', securing the backing of American philanthropic groups, particularly that of CARE, the Co-operative for American Remittances to Everywhere (originally the 'E' stood for Europe). The venture, advertised as 'a citizen offensive against communism', linked up usefully with Magsaysay's decision to concentrate his presidential campaign on the neglected rural areas. Between 1953 and 1956, eleven rural community centres were opened, equipped with radios, books, and sports equipment given by CARE. They served as useful beacons for Magsaysay, and after his election he reiterated his determination to focus attention upon the neglected rural areas. But the NAMFREL venture was by no means the only tool for his purpose. Indeed, Magsaysay first inclined to favour the Philippine Rural Reconstruction Movement, with its internationally-known guiding genius, Dr Y. C. James Yen.

Dr Yen, after education at Yale, began working in the field of adult education during the first world war. His experiences in north China led him to believe that the 'four fundamental weaknesses' of Chinese life—ignorance, poverty, disease, and civic disintegration—must be 'tackled in a correlated manner'. His work attracted American support, and in 1928 a Committee for Mass Education was formed in the United States. In 1948 Dr Yen succeeded in obtaining a grant of $27,500,000 (being 10 per cent of all American aid to China) for his rural reconstruction work; after the communist revolution he transferred his activities to Formosa. In 1952 he launched PRRM, to make the Philippines the 'demonstration nation' for Asia, to show that 'economic sufficiency and political democracy can be achieved on Asian soil by an Asian people'. He was backed by the International Committee of the Mass Education Movement, New York, *Reader's Digest*, and other powerful interests. In April 1954 Yen was asked by President Magsaysay to take responsibility for the San Luis Project (a rehabilitation scheme for an area recaptured from the Huk insurgents: the home-town of the Huk leader, Luis Taruc) in Pampanga Province, central Luzon. Yen's technique is known in Community Development jargon as 'intensive': he concentrates massive resources within a limited area, so as to achieve a total impact upon the local society and its economy. By June 1959 there were thirty-two government agencies and twenty-five voluntary organisations at work in the San Luis area and (according to a perhaps over-critical calculation) expenditure had totalled 3,260,000 pesos.[3]

Dr Yen needed to emphasise the Filipino character of his organisation. Magsaysay, like most of his countrymen, regarded the Chinese as synonymous with economic exploitation. Yen took as his partner Senator Tomas Cabili, a confidant of the president, and in their joint names a Three-Year Rural Reconstruction Plan was laid before Magsaysay. Its total estimated cost was over $40 million. Carrying presidential credentials, Yen and Cabili went off to Washington to get the money.

Meanwhile, President Magsaysay set up a Community Development Planning Council, which first met in January 1955. This was a heads-of-departments committee, and its members were by no means united in support for the new venture; several were much more concerned to safeguard their own departmental welfare projects. The only whole-hearted enthusiast for a new organisation was the council's secretary, Ramon Binamira, a young lawyer without political influence who owed his rise to former campaign work for Magsaysay with NAMFREL. Binamira did enjoy the valuable support of a senior UN expert, Dr E. R. Chadwick, formerly a district officer in Nigeria. He later attracted the goodwill of Colonel H. A. Brenn, director of the United States Operations Mission.

In a general, diffused way, the president supported both Yen

[3] Before the revaluation of September 1960, 2 pesos = $1.

52

and Cabili in their efforts to get funds from the United States Congress for rural reconstruction, and also Binamira and Chadwick in their proposals for a Community Development department, supported by USOM. He appears to have hoped that both geese might lay golden eggs. At first it appeared that Yen would be successful in America, but after months of lobbying he was finally disappointed. Meanwhile, in December 1955, Colonel Brenn of USOM came through with the offer of $4 million for a programme on Binamira–Chadwick lines. Rural Reconstruction was off. Community Development was on.[4] At this point Magsaysay abolished the Planning Council and created an office of Presidential Assistant (PACD) with Binamira in charge. This new arrangement eliminated the political sniping of rival cabinet leaders, and gave the direct authority of the president to the new agency in its dealings with other government bodies. The actual impact of the president was scanty, both in the case of Magsaysay and of Garcia.

How then has PACD sustained its autonomy? It is a tasty morsel for the politicians, for, as Binamira himself has observed, 'Politics and handouts go together like rice and fish.' The main safeguard is the heavy American investment and interest. About 60 per cent of the PACD budget comes from the US government ($6 million for each of the years 1956–9 and 1959–60), while CARE and other private American bodies contribute generously in goods and equipment. The Presidential Assistant on Community Development finds itself in the dilemma that if it continues to lean on American aid it remains a give-away programme, while if it attempts to become nationally self-supporting it will then become vulnerable to political pressure.

Despite certain characteristics peculiar to Filipino society, the problems of the rural community are those which confront southern Asia in general. Three-quarters of the population live in the countryside in 19,000 *barrios* or village tracts. Nearly half the agricultural land is held under tenancy, and 63 per cent of the peasants

[4] The subsequent record of PRRM may be briefly told. As president of the International Mass Education Movement, Dr Yen still has powerful resources. During 1960, two new institutes were started, at a cost of millions of dollars, as centres of intensive effort in one hundred village tracts, mainly in Nueva Ecija, Luzon. For a full account of the PRRM/PACD tussle, see J. V. Abueva, *Focus on the Barrio* (Manila, 1959).

are tenants. Population is increasing at a rate of over 3 per cent per annum. Landlordism, small and fragmented holdings, low productivity, soaring population: these factors are inherent in the problem. Rural society is dominated by the landlords, the *hacenderos* or *caciques*, many of whom are absentees, dwelling at Manila or living in the *poblacion*, the urban centre of the municipality.[5] The impact of government services has scarcely penetrated into the rural *barrios*; apart from elementary schools, there are no other services, and 12,000 of the 19,000 *barrios* are not connected by road with the outside world. Power, to the peasants, is the prerogative of the landlord and his nominee the politician. The politician is interested from time to time in purchasing the rural vote at the price of some showy concession—a new school-house or an artesian well, maybe. This he will contrive from the government patronage at his disposal, the 'pork barrel', as it is universally called in the Philippines. The politician links his supporters to him by a ritual kinship known as *compadrazgo*. Originally a godfather, the *compadre* is no longer in any intimate relationship, he is a public man who gives favours to his 'kin' in return for their active support.

Community Development seeks to replace this patron-client polity by equal co-operation, and it emphasises the village as the level at which the bonds of fellowship are realised. The Filipino village, like the village throughout southern Asia, has a historic sense of unity, and even today forms the mould in which the peasant has his being. But is the village a unit in a positive sense? Great stress has been laid on the Filipino tradition of *bayanihan*, whereby, when a family desires to move house, their neighbours gather with stout bamboos and all together literally move the building to its new site. This co-operation or *lusong* is cited by Community Development publicists as an example of village combination. But traditionally the obligations of *lusong* are not owed to the village at large but to one's kinsfolk: moreover, this practice is dwindling as the direct dealings of old are replaced by the commercial transactions

[5] The Philippine municipality descends from Spanish days. It is a combined urban-rural administrative area, comprising the *poblacion* and perhaps ten to fifteen *barrios*; each *barrio* with a population of 2,000 to 5,000 or more. The *barrio* may be divided into *sitios* or hamlets. The headman is called *teniente del barrio*, the lieutenant; before 1960 he was appointed by the government.

of this day. The whole ethos of the contemporary Philippines is away from communal co-operation and towards individual enterprise.

The Community Development programme is, intendedly, based on self-help. At the ground-level is the 'multiple-purpose' village worker, who supervises three or more *barrios* and lives near by. His task is to help the village people to draft proposals for specific projects, to which the villagers bind themselves to contribute in cash, materials, or labour. This contribution is supposed to be equal to that of the government, and the 'fifty-fifty' or 'matching' principle is constantly underlined by the Community Development publicists. But it is the element which is most difficult to assess and most suspect: many foreign observers believe that on the majority of projects the villagers' contribution in labour is inflated in the official estimates so as to preserve the 'matching' principle inviolate.

How far do the projects represent the 'felt needs' of the people? Their actual wants are for immediate economic relief: fair prices, access to free markets, tenancy reform. The remedies propounded by the Community Development staff sometimes coincide with these wants (as in the provision of improved stock, tools, or seed-grains, by gift or at a discount) but more often they envisage longer-term benefits than the village folk themselves would work for: roads, community centres, wells. These benefits are accepted by the villagers—and they are ready to put some labour into them—because they are offered on advantageous terms. It is the 'give-away' aspect of Community Development which attracts them, rather than an urge to work for the community. Mr Binamira himself declares that the programme has achieved real success only where the political network does not operate and the pork barrel is not available. The *persona* of the village-level worker in this situation is important: how far is he regarded as one of themselves by the villagers, how far as an official? Much is made of the spirit of service among the workers. During his six months' training period the probationer receives no salary. The bureaucracy in the Philippines is (in Binamira's phrase) 'bloated', 'bursting at its seams', but nevertheless there is an abounding surplus of graduates and lawyers and a government post at 150 pesos per month is not without material attractions. It is a higher wage than that of the village schoolmaster, who is nearly always a graduate.[6] At least half the probationers are town-dwellers. Their training at the Los Baños institute is distinctly theoretical in content. Community Development techniques have been overwhelmingly modelled on American methodology: for example in the formulation of theories of group behaviour.[7] The probationer emerges from the course as yet another copy-book white-collar bureaucrat; friendly, a power for good, no doubt, but still an official, one who gives orders to others.[8]

The attempt to rehabilitate rural society through Community Development led to a belated recognition of the village as a unit of self-government. The political transformation of the Philippines during the twentieth century from a Spanish colony to an American-style democracy never penetrated as far as the villages. The *teniente del barrio* remained the sole link between the rural folk and the urban political bosses. In September 1955, Republic Act 1408 made provision for *barrio* councils which were to be chosen from heads of families. The measure was ineffective: the Act required council elections to be conducted by a municipal councillor—whose powers it would partly usurp; the council's functions were ill-defined, and there were no proper financial provisions. A second measure, Republic Act 2370 of 1959, came into force on January 1, 1960. It was designed to remove the previous defects, and it was named the *Barrio* Charter. There is a *barrio* assembly, comprising all the local electors. This assembly meets annually; it elects a council and scrutinises the *barrio* financial transactions. The council includes the *barrio* lieutenant, a *barrio* treasurer, four council members, and the vice-lieutenants, the heads of the *sitios*. All members have two years in office. The council has a formidable list of duties, but it also has definite financial powers, including the right to levy a small tax on

[6] The village-level worker's 150 pesos is even comparable with the salary of the chief official of the municipality, the mayor, who in smaller municipalities earns 215 pesos per month.

[7] The training methods in the Philippines provide a striking contrast to those in India, which are designed to make the entire Community Development staff familiar with the practical tasks that must be tackled in the village by 'getting their hands dirty'.

[8] This conclusion and others expressed in this essay are reinforced by the findings of Mary Hollsteiner, *The Dynamics of Power in a Philippine Municipality*, University of the Philippines, mimeo., n.d.

landed property. The yield from new taxation may not be large: only 65 per cent of the national tax assessment is actually realised, and many provincial collections are much lower.[9] The principal asset of the new councils will be the voluntary contributions of the peasants.

There is some evidence that the councils, led by the new elected *barrio* lieutenants, are doing distinctly better than their predecessors. Between one-third and a half of the *barrios* have been brought into the PACD programme. Much organised activity in the Philippines is likened by cynics to *niñgas cogon*, the flaring up of dried grass, to blaze brightly for a moment, and then to die. Community Development appears to be holding its own and to be acquiring a deeper value than that of the material benefits it dispenses. The rural community has a potential capacity for co-operation. Class distinctions are largely absent from the Filipino village, and leadership is associated with personal reputation and an ability to get things done rather than with ancestral prestige. All members of a rural community are prepared to work alongside their brethren, and the slacker is shamed by public opinion into contributing his share. Community Development in the Philippines is not yet a 'people's programme' as its publicists claim: but it does inspire genuine popular support. If one is unable to accept all the claims made for it, this is because the programme does nothing to tackle the basic evil of landlordism and little to ameliorate the equally fundamental problem of a soaring population. Nor, on the political plane, can one see it making any radical shift in the locus of political power, which will remain firmly in Manila and the provincial capitals.

THAILAND

The directive for rural development in Thailand came from the head of government. Both Marshal Phibun Songkram and Marshal Sarit Thanarat were dictators, but Buddhist dictators, wishing to promote meritorious works of social benefit. In addition, now that Thailand is the centre of international activity, the headquarters of

[9] For example, in Iloilo Province the collections of the real property tax varied from 44 per cent (1954) to 40 per cent (1958). See T. Firmalino, *Political Activities of Barrio Citizens in Iloilo as they affect Community Development*, University of the Philippines, mimeo., 1960.

UN agencies as well as of SEATO, it becomes necessary to demonstrate to outside observers that this is a progressive state, concerned with the welfare of its people.

The first major experiment in rural development was the land settlement scheme at Senatburi in central Thailand in the 1940s. Marshal Phibun planned to move the capital from Bangkok (associated with the reigning Cakkri dynasty) to the former capital Lopburi, as a means of enhancing his own prestige. In order to open the way thither through jungle country, and also to provide food supplies for the proposed capital, a major work of clearance and settlement was put in hand at Senatburi. The scheme languished after Phibun's downfall in 1945, but he revived it again ten years later during his second period of office. The total area designated for development is about a million acres. Nearly half this area has already been allocated to settlers. The holdings resemble homesteads in the American mid-west, rectangular blocks, aligned along highways. Each settler receives about ten acres; one-fifth is cleared beforehand, and he is given some support during the first difficult year. For five years he is on probation, and then if he has made good he is given a title to the land. To visit a section where the settlers have been on the land for five years is to learn a lesson in Samuel Smiles 'self-help'. Some settlers have built substantial houses and stockyards, they have planted orchards, and are part-owners of tractors or trucks. Others have barely succeeded in scratching a living. The whole accent is on the individual: there are, of course, no villages in the accepted sense, only a number of shopping centres. The essence of Senatburi is benevolent despotism. Control is ultimately exercised by the Ministry of the Interior through the Department of Public Welfare. The scheme can be utilised when public policy requires the movement of population (as the old kings shifted Mons or Malays from miles away). Recently, with the increasing congestion of traffic in Bangkok, it was decided to remove the bicycle-rickshaws or *samlors* off the streets. Fifty thousand *samlor* drivers thus became unemployed, and a sizeable proportion of them were sent off to Senatburi to begin new lives as agriculturalists.

A nationwide development programme was started in 1958, also under the aegis of the Ministry of the Interior, by means of a newly-formed Community Development Administration. A pilot scheme was launched, concentrating on three hundred villages in different parts of Thailand.[10] The second stage of the programme (which began in 1961) will see the extension of the programme throughout the Korat plateau, one of the most backward and isolated parts of Thailand. The initial pilot scheme was devised largely to gain experience and to train organisers. In consequence, the allocation was on a generous scale, by the standards current in southern Asia: one village-level worker was allocated to each participating village. These workers were seconded from the administrative civil service; they are men of about ten years' service, mainly graduates, holding the rank of deputy *nai amphur*.[11] The first contingent was selected with regard to their rural sympathies, and they were directed not to wear their uniforms while on this assignment. However, in a land where status and hierarchy are punctiliously regarded, the official, paternal character of their role cannot be disguised. Projects are worked out according to the matching principle, and economic benefits are accorded first priority: wells, irrigation tanks, roads, cottage industries. Within the restricted limits of the pilot scheme it was possible to consider each village as an individual case. For example, one village might be composed of a united family or clan, long established upon one central village site; such a community would be capable of embarking at once upon agreed combined enterprises with little preliminary encouragement. Another village (so considered in the administrative framework) might contain a number of hamlets and scattered dwellings, straggling across miles of countryside; it would be necessary first of all to link up the separated units by means of access roads and tracks. But physical inter-communication will provide no guarantee of social inter-communication. In this environment the village-level worker may be driven to exercise his official authority in order to achieve results.

The Community Development administrators are in a dilemma, one in which many officials with pioneer ideas find themselves. The majority of them sincerely believe in the new philosophy of mutual self-help; and the more liberal hope that, through the growth of village councils, Thailand will learn something of the processes of representative government which hitherto have so conspicuously

[10] Altogether, there are some 40,000 villages in Thailand.

[11] Assistant to the district officer. Thailand is divided into seventy-one provinces, *changwad*, rather like counties; these are sub-divided into 411 districts, *amphur*, rather like English rural districts.

failed to take root. But the majority of senior officials in general have no faith in Community Development. Most of the provincial governors (particularly those drawn from the police) firmly believe that the peasant likes to be told what to do and does not want to have to decide for himself. Community Development, therefore, has to prove itself to a hostile audience. It has to achieve tangible results. If the principle of 'helping the people to help themselves' is patiently followed, results may be slow in coming: the temptation is strong to hustle the peasant, to get results, so as to demonstrate the virtues of self-help. It is not without significance that, in the villages first included in the pilot scheme, the first substantial project was the building of an elaborate village hall. Made of imported materials, constructed not because of the wishes of the villagers but through the will of the government, the community centre stands as a visible monument to the merit of Community Development. Only a cynic would call it a monument to *moha*, illusion.

Village leadership is still largely traditional in form. The *poo yai ban* or headman is normally chosen by the people from a family of hereditary village leaders, though the choice will not fall upon one lacking in personal qualities. His enterprise or conservatism will be a major factor in forming the local attitude to development. Of equal or greater importance will be the disposition of the abbot of the local monastery, if this stands close by. If the abbot will bestow his blessing upon Community Development, or even more—as in some villages—if he is prepared to take the lead in organising the work, then much may be achieved, especially in social betterment.

How far is Community Development likely to succeed in awakening a spirit of local independence? The *poo yai ban* and the elders are learning to speak up more boldly to visiting officials, and to regard themselves as coadjutors of the officials in the advancement of village welfare. Villages which have taken part in the pilot programme and benefited thereby have shown themselves ready to act as missionaries of mutual self-help to their neighbouring villages. But the village folk still look mainly to a beneficent government for the boons which will transform their life of toil. The Thai villager is self-reliant enough in the task of earning his daily bread, but he is a long way from comprehending that he is the original source of the dominion of his rulers and their power over him; authority has still a tinge of the divine.

The Malayan approach has been directly related to the overall national situation. Originally, Community Development was promoted as a counter-measure to the communist terrorists in order to demonstrate that the government had a positive answer to communist propaganda. After the terrorists were defeated and the country became independent under the Alliance government, development retained its vital importance; thereby the voters could be assured of the tangible benefits of the moderate, multi-racial Alliance policy.

Malaya began with the advantage of a general standard of living above that of the Philippines and Thailand. The canker within its body is the division between Malays and Chinese. The former live in their traditional settlements, the *kampongs*, and the latter dwell largely in the towns. Even where the two races are physically contiguous, as in some of the new villages created during the Emergency, they form two separated halves, with their opposites dwelling 'the other side of the track'.

In its initial plans, the government (still, of course, a British colonial administration) concentrated on the need to knit together the two races, and to overcome the barriers between government and people. At a conference of senior officials held in 1954, the concept of the community was defined: 'a community is a group of persons, not necessarily a racial or religious group, living within a geographical area and having certain interests in common', their report declared.[12] It went on to indicate that in Malaya this definition could not be applied. It found that the prevailing forces in rural society were a spirit of individualism, a lack of civic sense, a tendency to regard the government as a 'milch cow', traditionalism, racialism, illiteracy, and lack of leadership. A department of Community Development was established, and a programme of village self-help on orthodox lines was set up. A second conference, held in 1958, produced a diagnosis similar to that of its predecessor. Alarm was expressed at the disintegration of the *kampongs* and at the flight of the younger men into government service and into the towns. The continuing estrangement of governmental authority

[12] *Report on Community Development in the Federation*, Kuala Lumpur, 1954, pp. 3, 7.

61

from the mass of the population was restated: the *penghulu*, the headman, although a villager, was regarded by his fellows only as the representative of the government. Their confidence was reserved for the *ketuah*, the village elders.[13]

Another type of development commenced with the creation of the Federal Land Authority in 1956, having the task of opening up virgin jungle to cultivation. Within four years fifteen major schemes had been initiated. The largest of these were the Bilut scheme in the dense interior of Pahang State, covering 14,000 acres and giving land to 600 families, and the Sungei Tiang scheme in Kedah, planned to provide 500 families with 13,000 acres of land. These projects are conceived throughout in terms of benevolent paternalism. The settler undertakes as part of his agreement to develop the land under the instructions of the manager and his staff, and he agrees that if he fails to comply with instructions or is guilty of misconduct he 'may be required to vacate the land. The decision of the management authority will be final and binding.'

Independence arrived in August 1957, and was followed in the next two years by elections to the federal legislature and the state councils. The Alliance was confirmed in office, but not without growing signs of opposition, including the advent to power of the chauvinist Pan-Malayan Islamic party in the east coast states of Kelantan and Trengganu. The Alliance interpreted these results as a challenge, and made radical changes in its approach to national development. It was decided that the best means of retaining the people's confidence would be to promote a rapid and perceptible increase in material prosperity, particularly among the rural electorate whose vote is decisive. If all communities share in this rising prosperity (so the argument runs) this will serve to eliminate the main cause of racial discord (economic inequality) and validate the moderate Alliance policy.

Community Development, with its emphasis on evolutionary self-help and social healing, had no part in this new approach. The Community Development Department was dissolved, and the term itself disappeared from the administrator's vocabulary. Tun Abdul Razak bin Hussein, the vigorous deputy prime minister, became minister of Rural Development, with responsibility for the Federal

[13] *Report on the Conference on Community Development*, Kuala Lumpur, 1958, p. 24.

Land Authority and for a new national development campaign of 'Immediate Results' projects. In each district, rural development committees were formed, composed of the district officer, technical heads of services, the local legislators, and representatives of the *kampongs*. Each committee was ordered to compile a District Rural Development Plan, the *Red Book*, as it is universally called in Malaya.

The *Red Book* is laid out exactly like a military operational order, and this is exactly what it is intended to be. District administration in Malaya was transformed by the Emergency. The district headquarters contained an operations room with a huge wall-map showing the security situation, and this was kept posted up to the minute as reports came in. Daily, or twice daily, meetings were held between the district staff, the security forces, and other services to co-ordinate their operations. If an administrative or technical road-block was encountered, concerted action could be taken to clear it away. Now, the drive generated by the Emergency is being transferred to development.

In an introduction to the *Red Book*, the minister defines the objectives as (1) the improvement of existing *kampongs* and (2) the opening up of new areas of land with new *kampongs*. It is laid down that 'Rural Development planning and subsequent action on the Plan takes priority over all other work in the district' and, in conclusion, all are informed: 'RESULTS ARE WHAT WE WANT'.

As regards the relationship between the government and the public, the *Red Book* has this to say:

(1) In a country such as ours, which possesses advanced technical resources, improvements in material amenities must very largely depend upon the application of these technical resources.

(2) There is little scope for active public participation in public works such as the construction of roads or bridges, the extension of water supplies, etc.

(3) All these must be left in the hands of government's own technical services.

In present circumstances, in Malaya, the sphere of activity in which the principles of Community Development can most valuably be applied is in the raising of morale among [*sic*] the individual *ra'ayat* [cultivator] and inducing in him a sympathetic attitude towards progress as a whole and in particular to progress by the application of technical agricultural knowledge—and hard work—ON HIS OWN LAND.

In these few sentences the ethos of mutual help and communal effort as it has been evolved by United Nations experts and others is totally rejected, and the emphasis put squarely upon technical expertise and individual effort.

The District Rural Development committees have been instructed by the minister 'not to consider whether or not funds will be available': 'do not worry at the planning stage as to what the total estimate of proposals comes to'. The district plans are forwarded to the State Development Committee and, after consolidation, the state plan is submitted to the federal Ministry. Trengganu and Kelantan, the Pan-Malayan Islamic Party states, have refused to co-operate with the federal government in development; but all the remaining states have received generous consideration of their requirements. Some districts have even been invited to put up more ambitious proposals. The buoyant Malayan economy permits planning to be governed by requirements and not by financial limitations. The only stipulation the minister makes is to require action—now. The *Red Book* declares that 'the key to Rural Development is an adequate network of access roads . . . capable of taking heavy lorry traffic in all weathers'. For example, in promoting rural education the accessibility of existing schools to the surrounding areas is the first consideration. Other improvements are designed to increase marketing facilities. The ultimate purpose is to build up a rural middle class by raising up the ordinary *ra'ayat* to this level, especially by the expansion of 'back-yard' rubber culture on holdings of ten acres each. Planning is based on the assumption that rubber will hold its present value in the world market. If this calculation proves to be well-based, then the ten-acre farmers (who at the beginning are being heavily subsidised) will become self-supporting within six years, and thereafter will enjoy real prosperity. It seems probable that the plans of the Alliance leaders will succeed in material terms; but little will have been done to alleviate the social maladies to which the earlier Community Development programme gave attention.

The division between Chinese and Malays will be perpetuated.

As one small example, a clearance scheme by the Sungei Tekali river, in the Ulu Langat district of Selangor state, may be cited. The cleared land lies deep in jungle and was for long a terrorist hide-out. When the forty specially-chosen families moved into their new homes they formed not one community, but two, Chinese and Malays, neighbours, united in a pioneer enterprise, yet separated into twin hamlets as though locked in some primordial feud.

And how far will Rural Development serve to bridge the gulf between government and people? The ministers may be assiduous in touring round the *kampongs* and in addressing gatherings of the *ra'ayats*; some, like the prime minister, will gain the respect and even affection of their audiences. But just as much as the administrators they will remain Olympian beings, far removed from the circle of acceptance of the *kampong*.

Unlike most of the institutions which the West has exported to Asia—such as systems of law, government, or education—the idea of Community Development is specifically formulated in relation to the social and economic character of Asia itself. Western society has not experimented with Community Development (except briefly in the Israeli *kibbutz*) and shows no inclination to sample its medicine. Community Development, as it has been conceived by most British administrators, Chinese social workers, American professors, and United Nations experts, is an attempt to graft western doctrines of behaviour on to a somewhat romantic or idealised notion of Asian village society. When Asian governments took over the dogma of Community Development and put it into practice, a new synthesis might have emerged, predominantly Asian in quality. In two of the countries surveyed in this paper, the Philippines and Thailand, the copy-book methodology has been retained intact, leading to strange disharmonies between theory and practice. In the third example, Malaya, the entire theory of mutual help and village combination has been modified in favour of an attempt to raise levels of income by a direct application of the mixed state direction and individual enterprise which the western countries favour for themselves.

The central problem—defined by J. S. Furnivall[14] as enabling the emergent peoples to 'want what they need, and do what they want'—still remains to be solved.

[14] In *Colonial Policy and Practice*, Cambridge, 1948, p. 470.

4

Climacteric in Asia

WHEN we learn history at school, history means dates: '1066 and all that'. Later we become more sophisticated and see the past in terms of movements, influences, trends. But some dates cannot be ignored: in Europe, for example, 1453, 1588, 1683, 1789, 1870, 1914. These were milestones, turning-points, when Europeans (whether they knew it or not) were acquiring a new future. Most people forget 'the lessons of history' when they leave school, but the immediate past, at any rate, is remembered; often in terms of decades to which labels (the Naughty Nineties, the Roaring Twenties) can be attached. It seems unlikely that destiny abets this fancy by arranging for significant events to fall near the turn of the decade; for Queen Victoria's death to close the nineteenth century, or the second world war to usher out the 1930s; but somehow it is these opportunely-timed events which we especially remember.

This is a somewhat laboured approach to the reflection that Asia has just passed a major milestone and will certainly remember the 1950s as a coherent and distinct period of time. The 1940s witnessed the rebirth of Asia. The 1950s may be termed the post-colonial period. There was a turning away from all that colonialism symbolised, and in world affairs this was the era of *pancha shila*; yet for most of the decade the leaders of the political parties and political institutions were mostly carried over from the colonial days. Then a spectacular change came over South and South-East Asia, internally and internationally. 1958–9 was a climacteric as important as 1947–9 or 1904–5 . . . 'And the new sun rose, bringing the new year.'

After independence, one of the most immediate surprises in

southern Asia was that so much remained the same. Most Englishmen, even those of a liberal persuasion, had expected independence
to lead directly to anarchy; the spectre of the tribesmen descending
from the hills, looting and burning, was a favourite theme: in the
words of Lord Bryce, 'To India severance from England would
mean confusion, bloodshed, pillage.'[1] At the other extreme, nationalist leaders confidently anticipated that independence would liberate
the genius of the people and bring a new millennium. On the eve of
independence U Nu declared, 'I shall predict that within five years
at the longest, this country of Burma ... will see once again such a
golden age.'[2] The premonitions of disaster were not entirely false:
division and disorder lay ahead of Burma, Vietnam, Punjab. But
even where the change-over was marked by violence, a surprising
degree of continuity was maintained. In Burma there was still the
deputy commissioner at the head of the district administration and
a district and sessions judge in the courthouse: shadows of their
British predecessors maybe, but still to the common people symbols
of authority. Similarly in Indonesia, the Dutch Residents had gone,
but Indonesians sat on in their place. In India, Pakistan, Ceylon and
Malaya there was a great deal more substance than shadow in the
continuance of former colonial practices. It was not, perhaps, surprising that judges, officials, and soldiers tried to keep up old ways,
absorbed through *esprit de corps*. But it was surprising when the
nationalist politicians carried on much the same. New Delhi was
completed just in time for the Indian National Congress leaders to
move in; the new president into the Viceroy's House, the new
premier into the residence of the commander-in-chief; the scarlet-
coated bodyguard, the ceremonial remained unchanged. Similar
house-warmings took place throughout southern Asia. Along with
the style and trappings of the departed Europeans, the nationalist
leaders took over their technique of government, over-centralised,
autocratic, aloof, and they found themselves forced to acquiesce in
a great deal of colonial policy and practice.

[1] James Bryce, *The Ancient Roman Empire and the British Empire
in India*, London and New York, 1914, p. 77. More surprisingly, Arnold
Toynbee was still anticipating a similar breakdown in the 1930s: *A Study
of History*, London and New York, 1936, Vol. V, p. 466.
[2] Cited in Tinker, *The Union of Burma, a Study of the First Years
of Independence*, London and New York, 3rd ed., 1961, p. 94, n. 2.

For some time, ordinary life in southern Asia went on much the same, as a clock continues to tick away after the one who wound it up has gone. There was a dual impulse: the colonial legacy of an army, civil service, and police, and the anti-colonial political leaders. Both elements were headed by a middle-class, western-educated élite. Many had of course been bitter opponents of colonialism, but they were none the less indelibly impressed by western ideas; 'brown Europeans' they are aptly called. In some states (notably Pakistan) the civil service and army element were more solidly established than the politicians. Elsewhere (especially in Burma and Indonesia) the politicians outweighed a weak public service. Only in India was there something like a balance, with politicians and public servants respecting the function of the other. The countries which had passed through Japanese occupation acquired a further factor in the national equation: the leaders of the guerrilla resistance. In Malaya and the Philippines, the resistance was eventually, after prolonged struggle, absorbed, outmanœuvred or liquidated. But in Vietnam, Burma and Indonesia the resistance was still a major force: the leaders penetrated both politics and the army, and created an 'erratic' factor in the pattern of power.

The post-colonial period, or the colonial epilogue as it is visualised in this essay, was distinguished by the continuing predominance of the pre-independence Freedom movements: the Congress in India, the AFPFL in Burma, and others were, in their own estimation and that of the general public, far more than political organisations. They represented the national will, the soul of the people, the means of liberation from bondage. Pre-independence unity, forged out of opposition to colonialism, had managed to disguise political, social, and religious differences (though not the differences between Gandhi and Jinnah). After independence, the Freedom movements found a certain unity in continued attacks on colonialism. For Indonesia this was specific: an obsession with the wrongs of the Dutch. For India, Burma, and Ceylon it was general, an assault on imperialism at large. For Pakistan, the obsession was not British but Hindu 'imperialism'. The Freedom movement leaders had encouraged their supporters to expect a new and better world after independence (the 'revolution of rising expectations'). But apart from foreign policy, dynamic change was hard to find.

Writers frequently allude to the post-colonial régimes as 'revolutionary'.[3] How far is this justified? Revolution implies at least a shift in power from one group to another. Of course, the European overlords departed, and their allies (some might say creatures) the aristocracy, notably the princes in India and the regents in Indonesia, were rapidly stripped of the vestiges of their power. But the change was less spectacular than it appeared. Political initiative, a large measure of economic control, and the whole substratum of administrative authority were already within the hold of the Asian westernised middle class. Nowhere was there a social revolution on the Russian pattern. Neither was there, to any significant extent, an ideological revolution, despite the manifold references to Marx. The Left, of course, was concerned with adapting Marx to Asian circumstances; but the new governments were actually motivated by a mixture of inherited political concepts; the mixed authoritarianism and liberalism which had imbued (and confused) the European imperialists were combined with traditional Asian religious and social doctrine.

Everywhere, the Freedom movement leaders took office with high ambitions, yet they found themselves dealing with the same basic problems as their colonial predecessors, often compelled to accept the same solutions. Planning had a great vogue, but the plans did little more than adjust pre-existing schemes within an articulated framework: this was precisely the scope of the First Indian Five Year Plan. When the planners tried to formulate radical innovations (as in the American KTA economic plan for Burma) they succeeded in achieving little more than a paper success. The schemes for land reform in southern Asia were mostly directed at eliminating the absentee landlord: another measure to deflate a group which had already ceased to exercise any effective social leadership. Under land reform, working tenants acquired a more substantial title, some absentee landowners were obliged to assume a less nominal interest in their land to retain their estates, but there was little redistribution of the soil to new cultivators. The landless labourers were landless still. And co-operative or collective farming was talked about but not practised. Even in India, where idealism and administrative talent were most harmoniously combined, the drag of the past could not, seemingly, be overcome. There was the revolution that failed in

[3] Cf. Ba Swe, *The Burmese Revolution*, Rangoon, 1952.

the countryside. In pursuit of the Gandhian ideal of village republics, autonomous councils were set up throughout the land. Subsequently, the wider problem of rural stagnation was tackled by a programme of economic rehabilitation. The villagers were called upon to band together as communities; in support, there would be government advisers, technicians, and grants. After twelve years, the village councils were almost everywhere described as moribund, and the Community Development programme, far from arousing village initiative, had been sustained only by direction from above by officials of the district administration. Government and the governed have remained two separate and distinct categories, as in colonial or pre-colonial days.

The one sphere where change was noticeable was in foreign policy. From 1784 to 1942, the Indian Ocean was a British–Indian lake. With the coming of independence and the withdrawal of the Royal Navy and the Indian Army from their protective role, the leaders of the new Asian nations made it clear that they intended to forge an independent position in world affairs. At Bandung in 1955 they gathered together to enunciate this position under the sign of *pancha shila*. This independent, uncommitted viewpoint was most effective in terms of a solid bloc of votes in the United Nations; yet, largely through Indian initiative, *pancha shila* also made a vital contribution to the Korea peace settlement and the Geneva agreement on Vietnam. Was there a somewhat artificial quality about these developments? The description of the territories evacuated by the European powers as a 'power vacuum' is often depreciated as evidence of the imperialist mind; but it is difficult to avoid talking of a vacuum in southern Asia in the 1950s. The example of the futility of Dutch and French attempts to cling to power served to persuade the West of the advantages of disengagement, while the communists did not yet appear to regard the time as ripe for intervention. India also saw more benefit in a Good Neighbour policy of non-interference in her areas of economic activity in South-East Asia; while Indonesia, the Philippines, and the rest were in no position to attempt to extend their influence. But if the success of *pancha shila* depended upon various kinds of involuntary self-denying ordinances, it was none the less significant as the only attempt to formulate an alternative to deadlock between the communist and the 'free' worlds.

The southern Asian governments which sent their delegates to the Bandung Conference in 1955 were still established on a Freedom movement base. Almost immediately, signs of change appeared. In 1956, the United National Party in Ceylon was ousted by a Leftist coalition; the dominance of the Muslim League in the central government of Pakistan dissolved; the Nationalist (PNI) government in Indonesia ceased to command confidence; and in Burma the first rifts appeared in the AFPFL supremacy. Only in India did the Congress emerge from a second national General Election with its mandate undiminished. The rejection of the Freedom movements, and the splintering apart of parties elsewhere, led abruptly to political chaos or military rule. Can we explain this apparently sudden collapse of governments which had been accepted as the embodiment of the national will? And why did India not go the same way?

In part the answer lies in the unparalleled organisation of the Congress. No other Asian party, even in the Philippines, can offer any comparison. In part the difference is explicable in the degree to which the Congress movement under Gandhi established a hold in the minds of the mass of the people. But part of the answer must be ascribed to the luck of survival or demise among national leaders. India has been supremely fortunate in both respects. Of all the services Gandhi rendered to his country, perhaps none was greater than the manner of his dying, which halted the massive forces of religious intolerance in India; certainly for the present, and perhaps for all time. Gandhi died: Nehru lived, to lead his people—their prince, priest, father, brother. In after years Nehru lost his delicate sense of public feeling, increasingly isolated from reality by his sycophantic 'court'. Yet his leadership was still unchallengeable to his death. In direct contrast, Pakistan lost its paramount leader after the nation's first year; and Jinnah, the realist, the pragmatist, created no effective political mystique for others to follow. His successors were sick men, men who were murdered, political jugglers. Pakistan's story might have been quite different had Jinnah been ten years younger or in robust health. Similarly in Burma and Ceylon: Aung San was killed even before the transfer of power; Don Senanayake died before a psychological adjustment to independence had occurred. Power slipped into the hands of men less determined and less clear-sighted. However, it is an oversimplification to explain everything in terms of a personality cult or 'charismatic leadership' as it is now fashionably termed. U Nu was compelled to relinquish the premiership although his personal popularity with the masses was undimmed. Sukarno still stands in the spotlight of leadership, but effective power has passed into the hands of the generals. Charismatic leadership, so called, appears to create a situation in which once initiative has slipped out of the grasp of the leader it cannot be snatched back.

The decline from grace of the Freedom movements may be further ascribed to two principal causes. Both are concerned with the outcome of democracy in Asia today. One concerns the subject-matter of politics. The political climate is no longer determined by the western-educated, the 'brown Europeans', but by the masses, still swayed by the forces of tradition. The second change is in attitudes to political institutions of western origin. After ten years' experience of what is often called 'fifty-one per cent democracy', many responsible Asians standing outside the political arena have come to question the whole logic of parliament and the ballot box. They do not agree that politicians who secure a parliamentary numerical majority (often on a minority of the popular vote) have an automatic mandate to govern the nation. They are particularly concerned at the division and strife which this system seems to encourage, both at the national and the local level.

The 'broadening down' of politics has begun to have its effect throughout South and South-East Asia except, as yet, in the Federation of Malaya, Thailand, South Vietnam—and possibly the Philippines. There a small upper middle-class group still holds the political initiative. But in most of the area the frame of politics has altered. The guiding principle of the Freedom movements was that of nationalism: nationalism in revolt against foreign rule. As we have seen, after independence this external force was effective in helping to shape foreign policy (where popular feeling was not, in the main, interested) but this force ceased to have any relevance for internal politics. Leadership still remained with the westernised middle class with their genuine sense of national unity, but their mandate was derived from the mass electorate to whom the idea of national unity was dim. The masses were concerned with issues arising out of older community loyalties formed by religion, the tribe, caste, or language. The latter identification acquired significance where the language of the European overlord was dismissed from use in administration, politics, and the educational system. Burma and Vietnam were able fairly easily to turn to established national languages (though in Burma important minorities were thereby alienated). Almost every other ex-colonial country had to make a choice of a tongue which would be foreign to a large minority (in India, a large majority) of the nation. In reaction, local linguistic patriotism based upon a regional or communal language was stimulated. This regional patriotism is often marked by antipathy to a neighbouring group, reviving historical rivalries, based in some cases on religious divisions.

Political controversy since about 1956 has increasingly focused upon these local or sectional issues as the parties have directed their appeal to the mass electorate. Leftist politicians in Ceylon have exploited the introduction of Sinhalese as the official language, with appeals to Buddhist sentiment, as popular issues to mobilise feeling against the Anglicised leaders of the UNP, and the economically more advanced Tamil (Hindu) minority. In this situation the non-westernised lower middle class, the shopkeeper, the *bhikku* or Buddhist monk, and the village schoolmaster have become figures in politics. Policy has been harnessed to the emotions of the under-privileged. The susceptibility of the mob in Pakistan to the cry 'Islam in danger' was cynically exploited by party leaders, leading to the total breakdown of law and order in Lahore and other cities in 1953, and causing the first intervention by the army into the political arena to enforce martial law. Separatist movements in Burma have been aroused by the feeling among certain groups, particularly the Karens, Shans, and Arakanese, that they are regarded as second-class citizens. Extremists both of the Right and the Left in India have appealed to religious prejudice (Hindus versus Christians in Kerala, for example) or local consciousness, as in communist exploitation of the demand for the inclusion of the city of Bombay in the Maharashtrian state. In India, despite certain lapses, the Freedom movement leaders have succeeded in conciliating or quelling these demands based on popular prejudice; but in Pakistan and Ceylon the politicians found themselves victims of their own attempts to cash in on prejudice. From being the leaders they became the led.

The spectacle of the politicians trying to ride the tiger, thereby dragging their nation into chaos, has discredited the name of democracy. When the proceedings of the East Pakistan legislature degenerated into a chair-throwing fracas in which the deputy speaker was killed, this exhibition was, by some, blamed upon the institution of parliament.

Some of the politicians themselves began to have second thoughts about the suitability of the parliamentary system for Asia, notably S.W.R.D. Bandaranaike in Ceylon and Jayaprakash Narayan in India. Both of them glanced at Switzerland with its loose federation of cantons and communes, but both insisted primarily on an Asian solution to the dilemma. There was a much more insistent demand for change from outside the political ranks, from business men, civil servants, and army officers. Of these only the army was in a position to make any effective protest. Everywhere in southern Asia (except in non-militaristic Ceylon) the army is strong and broad-based.

The Freedom movement leaders, of whom so many were lawyers, took it for granted that the military was subordinate to the civil power; but this was a minority view. Within the traditional pattern of authority there was no clear division between civil and military, and in Mughal India the high officials, the *mansabdars*, ranked on a basis of military command. The western colonial governments had a distinctly military tinge; even in the Philippines under American rule, military men were appointed to high office; French Indo-China was almost the creation and preserve of the French Navy; in India, Burma, and Malaya, military officers were frequently appointed as governors and in other civil posts until recent years. At the highest level of the government of India there was an undercurrent of conflict between civil and military authority which occasionally flashed into open challenge (Napier versus Dalhousie, Kitchener versus Curzon). Lord Bryce observed after visiting India, 'It is a military society, military first and foremost, though with a small infusion of civilian officials . . . lawyers, and merchants.' British India 'smells of gunpowder', he concluded.[4] This, then, was a factor which the politicians ignored at their peril. It was true that in Burma and Indonesia the new armies lacked the immense prestige and weight of the long-established forces of India and Pakistan; but they inherited a dynamic element which more

[4] James Bryce, *op. cit.*, pp. 13–14.

74

than compensated for the absence of tradition—the resistance element, many of them in high command, a 'band of brothers' who remembered that they had fought for freedom with guns when the politicians had been fighting with words.

And so the military risings against the politicians proceeded from two separate points of interest. The army leaders in Pakistan were conservative, the force of order; they intervened to restore efficient administration and correct standards of public conduct. Events in Thailand in 1958–9, the consolidation of the rule of Marshal Sarit Thanarat, so far as they related to any political philosophy were a similar expression of the force of order. But the army leaders in Burma and Indonesia were, to some extent at any rate, revolutionaries—the force of change, intervening to rekindle the spirit of the resistance.

Indian political leaders sometimes assume a little smugly that their country stands in a class apart in this matter: speaking at a symposium held in Delhi in December 1958, the speaker of the Lok Sabha referred to his country as 'the last remaining democracy in Asia'. Yet the army already exercises a great deal of thinly disguised power in India (especially in Kashmir) and it is not difficult to imagine a combination of circumstances in which people would turn to the army for salvation: for example, if the newly devised experiment in democratic Community Development should fail to yield a bonus in better living, or if the handling of the border dispute should fail to halt Chinese incursions into Indian territory. India is by no means clearly through the military take-over epidemic.

The India–China dispute is only the most spectacular evidence of the eclipse of *pancha shila*. Asia is unlikely to be heard again speaking in unison. Foreign policies are being painfully reset on lines of interest and security. Burma and Indonesia, for example, have learned a lot about Chinese dealings since Bandung. The effect of these changes would appear to contribute to enlarging the vacuum in southern Asia. *Pancha shila* appears to have failed, but there is no move towards a policy of reinsurance with the West.

Both in their internal development and in their foreign relations, the countries of South and South-East Asia have entered a time of flux and uncertainty. The relative stability of the post-colonial epilogue is gone; violent social change may be on the way. Will the workers at length begin to play some part in trade unions,

75

local councils, even in legislatures, where at present they are without a voice? Or will the forces of order effect a counter-revolution, reviving the old colonial systems, but with native instead of foreign satraps? However, it is still far too soon to compose a requiem for democracy in Asia. If present trends suggest increasing emphasis upon sectional, religious, or caste interests, it is feasible to regard this as a necessary phase through which Asian society has to pass before the concept of national unity is accepted by the ordinary people. It is also encouraging that today's military despots speak about their role as that of 'guardians' during a reconstruction interlude, after which responsible government will be restored. Whatever happens, it is surely predictable that the final pattern of the 1960s will differ markedly from that of the 1940s and 1950s.

5

India Today
A NATION IN MAKING, OR BREAKING?

A Bibliographical Survey

WHAT features give the study of Indian nationalism a special
significance? India is more than a country. It is (as Toynbee
indicates in his system of classification) a civilisation. Moreover, it is
a civilisation which at different times in world history has formed a
meeting-place, a junction for universal ideas and movements. Some
empires are culturally autonomous, self-sufficient, surrounded by a
Great Wall of mental isolation, repulsing external influences as
manifestations of barbarism: China is such a culture. But, as Jawaharlal Nehru observed, India's 'peculiar quality is absorption, synthesis'. While receiving, India has continually been giving to the
world. Ancient India was the matrix of astronomy and mathematics.
Hindu-Buddhist civilisation reached outward, sending its missionaries across Central Asia and the Far East; laying an indelible
impression upon South-East Asia. During the centuries of Muslim
rule, northern India absorbed Persian and Arabic cultural, political,
and legal concepts; contributing in turn to the Islamic heritage.
Finally, during two hundred years of British rule, European and
Christian ideas and beliefs created a new, westernised élite; the
professional and commercial middle class.

This Indian middle class has assimilated western values, consciously and unconsciously, into the mainstream of its thought and

77

behaviour. Greek political thought, the Christian ethic, the Enlightenment philosophy of the Rights of Man, nineteenth-century belief in democratic parliamentary institutions: all these have been assimilated, in theory, and to a lesser extent in practice, within the fold of Hinduism. Indian nationalism is founded upon a political and social ethos, combining western and indigenous elements, of a range and depth beyond almost all the other national movements which have risen, meteor-like, in the post-war world. Whereas in most of these movements the 'modern' (represented by alien, western dogma) and the 'traditional' (the forces of custom, religion, and social pressure) form separate compartments of thought and behaviour, Indian nationalism is based upon political philosophies in which foreign and native influences have interacted and mingled: if they have not entirely merged. The Gandhian philosophy is, perhaps, the most complete illustration; it is based on two thousand years of Hindu thought, from the *Gita* onward; but it is even more profoundly marked by the teaching of the Sermon on the Mount, by Ruskin, Tolstoy, Kropotkin.[1] In his autobiographical *The Story of My Experiments with Truth*, Gandhi frames his thoughts in purely Hindu terms: he defines the purpose of his *Experiments* as to achieve self-realisation, to see God face to face, to attain *moksha* (enlightenment).[2] Yet, as he acknowledges, his Hinduism has been transmuted: he is influenced by concepts which have no place in ancient Hindu belief, such as humility, sin, salvation. By contrast, in his *Autobiography*, Nehru appears as one who is consciously secular in outlook, emancipated from the superstition of the past: yet he pursues a restless Byronic search for a philosophy. He confessed in *An Autobiography*: 'I have become a queer mixture of the East and West, out of place everywhere, at home nowhere.'[3] Twenty years later, he was still striving to reconcile the irreconcilable: liberalism

[1] See Joan V. Bondurant, *Conquest of Violence; the Gandhian Philosophy of Conflict*, Princeton, 1958. For an excellent conspectus of Indian thought from classical times to the present day, see *Sources of Indian Tradition*, compiled by W. T. de Bary, R. Weiler and A. Yarrow, New York, 1958.

[2] Gandhi, *An Autobiography: The Story of My Experiments with Truth*. Translated from Gujarati by Mahadev Desai, London, 1949.

[3] Jawaharlal Nehru, *An Autobiography*, London and New York, 1936 (over twenty reprints).

and Marxism, the spiritual and the material, nationalism and internationalism.

Indian nationalism, then, has emerged out of a process of fusion and fission. This development in the realm of ideas has been paralleled by a steady development in the practical experience of government and politics. Let us recall that the three great universities of Calcutta, Bombay, and Madras opened their doors in 1857. The first Indian became a barrister in 1862, G. M. Tagore; and the first Indian succeeded in the highly competitive examination for the superior Indian Civil Service in 1864, Satyendranath Tagore (both these pioneers came from the brilliant Calcutta family of whom Rabindranath Tagore is the most famous member). The Indian National Congress held its first session in 1885. These events of the middle years of the nineteenth century are reminders of long-term Indian participation in political institutions of a western character. In independent India, the legislature, the judiciary, the executive— as well as political parties and the press—are all established upon foundations which have stood, and been tested, over a long period. The evolution of these processes of political growth can best be studied in the reports of the commissions and committees which were appointed to consider the course of further political development.[4] Of these reports, perhaps the most notable was the last, *The Report of the Indian Statutory Commission*, usually known as the *'Simon Report'* from the name of its chairman. Whoever wishes to understand the setting in which the political forces contended for power and influence in the years before independence, should read its pages. The *Simon Report* describes how British rule had established 'the conceptions of impartial justice, of the rule of law, of respect for equal civic rights without reference to class or creed, and of a disinterested and incorruptible civil service'. The *Simon Report* takes account of 'the immense area and population of India, the diversities of race, creed, and caste' but insists upon the geographical, political, and economic unity of the subcontinent, and concludes: 'The unity imposed upon India by the external forces of Great

[4] Especially, *Report of the Royal Commission Upon Decentralisation in India*, London, 1909, ten vols; *Report on Indian Constitutional Reforms*, London, 1918; *Interim Report . . . Review of the Growth of Education in British India*, London, 1929; *Report*, etc., *of the Indian Statutory Commission*, London, 1930, seventeen vols.

Britain is today reinforced by an increasing sense of Indian nationality.' Nationalism is regarded as a unitary movement: '... The
one force in Indian society today that may perhaps contain within
itself the power to overcome the deep and dangerous cleavages that
threaten its peace.'

Within twenty years of the appearance of the *Simon Report*,
the subcontinent had been divided into two mutually hostile
nations. Nationalism had assumed a form contrary to that which
Indian political leaders had taken for granted for eighty years. The
unity of India had been an article of faith with all westernised
nationalists: yet, in the 1920s and '30s, as an increasing proportion of
the population was accorded the franchise, and in the shadow of an
imperial abdication, the most important Indian religious minority
decisively pronounced that the loyalties of its members lay with
religion and not with the geographical entity, India.

How did this association of nationalism with religion emerge?
Right up to the threshold of independence, most outsiders were
mystified by this gathering in of the Muslims. Why were the aristocratic, Persianised landlords of Oudh, the tough, martial peasantry
of Punjab, and the schoolmasters and cultivators of Bengal united
under the leadership of a cosmopolitan Bombay barrister? Why did
they demand a political solution which must banish a sizeable
minority of them to a permanent political wilderness? Some observers, like Nehru, dismissed the whole movement as obscurantist,
unnatural, unreal. Others suspected that the demand for Pakistan
was an elaborate red herring or ruse to obtain political concessions
of an entirely different order. Too late, the Congress leaders realised
that in frustrating and irritating the Muslim community by petty,
legalistic manœuvres they had contributed to making inevitable the
Partition of India: the consummation they so absolutely abhorred.
How did the Muslim demand acquire its irresistible momentum?
And how did the Congress come to place itself in the position of
contributing to the alienation of the Muslims? A satisfactory explanation of the Pakistan demand has only recently been given in
Khalid Bin Sayeed's *Pakistan, the Formative Phase*.[5] Professor
Sayeed disposes of several myths. He effectively demonstrates that
the legend of a British master plan to drive a wedge between Hindus
and Muslims ('divide and rule') is so much eye-wash. He also seeks

[5] Khalid Bin Sayeed, *Pakistan, the Formative Phase*, Karachi, 1960.

to modify the view that Pakistan was created by the iron will of one man, Mohammad Ali Jinnah. He argues that, although the Pakistan concept was defined by middle-class Muslim political theorists, it only became practical politics when the Muslim masses took up the slogan and raised the old cry of 'Islam in danger', sweeping along the secular, middle-class lawyer-politicians upon a wave of religious emotionalism. This mass agitation of the emotions among the Indian Muslims formed the first departure from the westernised middle-class political thought which (so we argue in this survey) provided the foundation of the Indian national movement. It is significant that with this eruption of traditional, irrational mass feeling, the *national* political impulse of the middle class is replaced by an identification with an older more narrow group loyalty. This trend, we shall see, recurs in independent India.

Interpretations of the events which led to Partition, written from the Congress viewpoint, do not give a satisfactory explanation of the Congress behaviour. The standard account is *The Transfer of Power in India*, by V. P. Menon.[6] The author was constitutional adviser to the viceroy during the crucial years 1942–7. His subsequent close association with the Congress central government, and Sardar Patel in particular, tinges his interpretation of events: though his general objectivity is beyond question. Another work which provides a detailed narrative of this period is Michael Brecher's *Nehru, a Political Biography*.[7] The author is a Canadian political scientist, but he would not deny that his sympathies are engaged by the subject of his portrait. The third book to be mentioned is the least *engagé*; R. P. Masani's *Britain in India* is a balanced, clear-eyed account of these times by one who was a compassionate observer of the struggle.[8] However, Mr Masani did not have access to confidential documents, while his own outlook is so liberal and free from fanaticism that he simply cannot grasp the nature of the Muslim demand.

Let us examine the situation. The Indian National Congress claimed that its title was a literal description of its role: that of the only body entitled to speak for all the peoples of India. Its members delighted to call their activities the 'Freedom movement': they were

[6] *The Transfer of Power in India*, London and Princeton, 1957.
[7] *Nehru, a Political Biography*, London and New York, 1959.
[8] *Britain in India*, Bombay, 1960.

no mere political party, they manifested the soul of India. The Congress leaders dismissed the pretensions of the Muslim League as the posturings of a British-created faction, a product of the policy of divide and rule. Congress was concerned with only one solution for India's political problems: *purna swaraj*, 'full independence'. British attempts to find constitutional formulae to safeguard the minorities were regarded as little more than devices for perpetuating imperial control. This remained the Congress position down to the closing months of 1946, when Nehru was still brushing aside the claims of the Muslim League and the proposals of the British alike. 'Our patience is fast reaching the limit', he threatened. 'If these things continue, a struggle on a large scale is inevitable.' Yet, within a few weeks, the Congress had acquiesced in such a settlement as had been theirs for the taking all along. They agreed to Dominion status within the framework of the Government of India Act of 1935, which Gandhi had pronounced 'satanic' (though he admitted he had not read it). More extraordinary, Congress agreed to the division of India.

How did all this come about? The three authors previously cited recite their narratives of the public events which led to this capitulation. They cannot expose the minds of the Congress leaders for us, and their motives remain hidden. Only one of the Congress inner circle has so far published his memoirs, Maulana Abul Kalam Azad, Congress president, 1940–5. His *India Wins Freedom* appeared posthumously in 1959, and created a furore.[9] Azad purports to explain how Congress came to accept Partition, by attributing the decision to personal and political mistakes and failures. His account is openly partisan. He does help to explain why Jinnah's attitude to the Congress (of which he was once an enthusiastic member) hardened into hatred. Azad artlessly reveals his own share in deliberately frustrating the Muslim League from achieving office in Punjab, when this was their right as the majority party in the legislature. At the same time, he condemns Nehru for going back upon agreements entered into with the League, in 1937 and again in 1946. He reveals how (largely at the instigation of Sardar Patel) the Congress leaders arranged that a Muslim Leaguer should be offered the portfolio of finance in the interim government, so that he should 'make a fool of himself' (p. 166). In fact, the League

[9] Maulana Abul Kalam Azad, *India Wins Freedom*, Calcutta, 1959.

finance minister, Liaqat Ali Khan, turned the tables upon his Congress colleagues.

Azad, as a staunch nationalist Muslim, opposed the idea of Pakistan to the end. He would have us believe that Lord Mountbatten was sent to India as viceroy with the express purpose of 'selling' the Pakistan solution to the Congress. Patel, we are told, was persuaded because he despaired of working harmoniously with Liaqat Ali as finance minister; Nehru agreed because Lady Mountbatten charmed him into agreement; and Gandhi gave way because the other two had already been persuaded! It is true that elsewhere Azad shows up the Congress leaders as political opportunists. But it is difficult to believe that they abandoned lifelong convictions so weakly.

Perhaps, under stress, the Congress leaders found themselves at odds with their ideologies. Gandhi had based his political action in *satyagraha*, 'soul force' (literally, sacrifice-firmness). On numerous occasions from 1922 to 1942 he had found to his dismay that his mass-following were unable to understand and practise *satyagraha*. It was a force that could be used to great effect by the dedicated few, but not by the ignorant many. Even Gandhi's political heir, Nehru, was not a whole-hearted believer in the doctrine. We find Nehru writing to Gandhi: 'For myself, I delight in warfare. It makes me feel that I am alive.'[10] Hence, Congress was always oscillating between moral force and physical force, which was contrary to Gandhian teaching. Violence was always being stirred up by Congress actions; but the liberal strain in their ideology checked the Congress leaders from ruthlessly exploiting violence; they held back from the consequences of their actions. Hence, paradoxically, the British administration was always able to suppress outbreaks of mob violence; yet, at the same period, British public opinion was gradually submitting to the moral persuasion of Gandhi, which created the impression that alien overlordship in India was no longer morally justifiable. *Satyagraha* had triumphed: yet in the hour of crisis, Congress could not invoke *satyagraha* as a mass instrument. Neither could it call upon the weapon of violence. Moreover, though Nehru believed himself to be a revolutionary, when the challenge came he was not prepared to adopt revolutionary measures: it was the liberal in him which supervened. He placed

[10] Quoted by Michael Brecher, *op. cit.*, p. 159.

himself at the head of the reformers, the moderates, and accepted self-government upon terms laid down by the British government and the Muslim League.[11] For—again it is a paradox—when the crisis came, Jinnah, the constitutional lawyer, the lifelong negotiator, was prepared to say 'The death of ten million Muslims is not too great a price to pay for Pakistan.' In the last resort Nehru was the prisoner of his liberal humanism; Jinnah was ready to throw away his liberalism and rely upon Islamic fatalism.

This, then, is the interpretation of the puzzling events of 1946–7 which this writer puts forward. It remains only a hypothesis. Perhaps, within a few years, the confidential documents of the negotiations which preceded independence will be opened up for scholarly investigation, and it may be possible then to complete the story. On the other hand, it may be found that no final interpretation can be construed from the documents: so much was decided by private consultation and unofficial dealing and was never recorded in official minutes. We do know of one example: Jinnah never formally accepted the Mountbatten plan for partition on behalf of the Muslim League. He only nodded his head in silence at the crucial moment in the negotiations.[12] Pascal bade us consider Cleopatra's nose as a factor in history; future scholars may be compelled to try to assess the historical consequences of Jinnah's nod.

With the attainment of independence, the first important national task was the drafting of a constitution. This has attracted a copious literature: studies of the constitution are still appearing. This concentration of attention upon the formal structure of government follows an established British scholarly convention. Such writers as Arthur Berriedale Keith and Sir Reginald Coupland (the first an academic lawyer, the second an historian) had studied Indian political development largely in terms of constitution-making, and

[11] Speaking in the Constituent Assembly in 1949, Sardar Patel claimed that he had demanded as the price of Congress agreement to Partition, first, that Britain should withdraw from India within two months, and second, that Britain would give Congress a free hand in settling the future of the Princely States. This claim has never (within this writer's knowledge) been repeated elsewhere. Azad specifically states that the decision to speed up the transfer of power was that of Mountbatten alone—Azad, *op. cit.*, p. 199.

[12] V. P. Menon, *op. cit.*, pp. 376–7.

Indian professors adopted the same pattern without question. Out of this library of constitutional studies, it will perhaps be sufficient to notice two works only.

The greatest responsibility for drafting the new constitution rested upon Sir B. N. Rau, adviser to the Constituent Assembly, 1946–9. A posthumous collection of his papers has been made by B. Shiva Rao.[13] Sir B. N. Rau (who later became a member of the International Court of Justice at The Hague) was a jurist of the highest calibre. He carefully scrutinised all possible precedents for the Indian constitution, which has both federal and unitary features. He was infused by a concept of citizenship broader than that of nationality. He laboured to keep India within the British Commonwealth of Nations, and he envisaged even wider concepts of international citizenship. Thanks to Rau, the Indian constitution has provided a firm framework for parliamentary democracy. Probably the best commentary upon the constitution is that of Alan Gledhill, a former High Court Judge in British Burma, and now professor of Oriental Laws in the University of London.[14] Besides providing a lucid exposition of the 395 Articles and nine Schedules which make up the longest constitution in the world, Professor Gledhill provides many interesting *aperçus* into its implications. Clearly, a system of government in an early stage of growth is greatly affected by the nature of those who are the first office-holders. In India, Nehru had been prime minister since independence: like a prince and priest in the eyes of his people, he dominated parliament and the nation as no western statesman has done: not even General de Gaulle. During these years, the office of president had been filled by the modest, pious Dr Rajendra Prasad. This personal juxtaposition caused most observers to regard the prime minister as the fulcrum of government in India, with the president solely a ceremonial head of state. However, Professor Gledhill demonstrates that a considerable reserve of power was entrusted to the president. These plenary powers were exercised only at the request of the prime minister and cabinet: the most notable occasions being the termination of the state governments in East Punjab, Andhra, and Kerala. A change in the balance of power is possible, for example if the prime minister

[13] Sir B. N. Rau, *India's Constitution in the Making*, ed. B. Shiva Rao, Calcutta, 1960.

[14] Alan Gledhill, *The Republic of India*, London, 1952.

lacked a commanding personality, or an overwhelming support in parliament and the nation. A later president might believe he was required actively to supervise the affairs of the nation, and perhaps, in the event of a parliamentary deadlock, actually assume charge of affairs. In such a situation, the roles of prime minister and president could be as decisively reversed as they were between the Fourth and Fifth Republics in France.

Meanwhile, parliamentary government in India remains unique in Asia. As late as 1930, the *Simon Report* declared that it was 'a difficult and delicate operation to transplant to India forms of government which are native to British soil'. Today, there are good reasons for believing that the plant has really taken root. A comprehensive study of parliament, its composition, machinery, rules, and actual working, has been made by W. H. Morris-Jones, Professor of Political Theory and Institutions at Durham University.[15] His book takes account of parliamentary activities up to 1954. In subsequent years, Professor Morris-Jones has somewhat modified his views and would probably now accord more importance to extraparliamentary forces. The concept of parliament in India as the central organ of government has been challenged by American political scientists as a 'formalistic' fallacy. They were inclined to dismiss parliament as little more than a sounding-board for Nehru and his associates.[16]

[15] W. H. Morris-Jones, *Parliament in India*, London, 1957.

[16] See, for example, N. D. Palmer and I. Tinker, "Decision Making in the Indian Parliament" in *Leadership and Political Institutions in India*, Princeton, 1959. The views of these critics would carry more weight if they clearly understood the role of the British parliament which they cite in contrast as the 'ideal' (p. 115) for that in India. They assert that parliament 'is the major agency for decision making' in a parliamentary democracy (p. 134). This is a purely 'formalistic' interpretation! In the British parliament, the majority party provides the government and controls policy; but the majority party in turn has to accept the leadership of the cabinet, and in a weak cabinet this means the leadership of the prime minister. Even by constitutional convention, the most vital 'decision making' is out of parliament's control: the declaration of a state of war, the dissolution of parliament itself, are decisions taken by the crown on the advice of the prime minister. And in less momentous decisions parliament can only follow the lead of the prime minister: for example, in the question of Britain's entry into the European Economic Community.

If we need to modify our assessment of the role of parliament in Indian politics this is not because of any inherent defect in the Indian operation of the institution. Parliamentary government everywhere is increasingly confounded by the growing technical complexity of our age, the acceleration of tempo in every kind of process, and by the tendency of government to become ever more involved in economic production and social welfare. Parliament is not easily adapted to these conditions. In addition, in India, parliament and the parties are having to adjust to a shift in the locus of political activity—a shift from a national debate down into a scuffle concerned with language, religion, caste, and class. The surprising aspect of the record of parliament in India is that it has functioned so well amid these pressures!

Morris-Jones shows how the procedure of parliament has already acquired its own usages at New Delhi and in most of the states. Westminster practices have been successfully assimilated, while India has evolved useful parliamentary techniques of her own, such as the Half-Hour Discussion Rule, whereby private members may raise issues after normal business. The Delegated Legislation Committee and the Assurances Committee are other means designed to permit the private member to keep the actions of the executive under surveillance. The tone of parliament is dignified and decorous, and in the minds of politically-conscious Indians it forms the 'Concourse of the Nation'. At certain moments (for example, after the communist invasion of Tibet) when Nehru's government failed to gauge the mood of the nation accurately, parliament spoke up as the voice of the nation's conscience. This is parliament's prime function: to provide a forum for discussion, for the declaration of aspirations, and for inquiry into discontents. There has been no great dialectical contest at New Delhi to compare with the slavery debates at Washington in the 1850s or the interminable dispute at Westminster over Irish Home Rule. This largely reflects the Indian sense that public opinion should be formed within a circle of agreement, rather than by aligning two sides in opposition. In almost every discussion upon the conduct of public affairs in India, the speakers will emphasise the importance of seeking unanimity. This concept has been called *sarvodaya*, or the 'uplift of all', and has been adopted as the essential basis of the political philosophy of Jayaprakash Narayan and his associates. Within such a system of belief it is not surprising that the party system has not established itself in popular esteem, and there is no organised opposition, such as the Anglo-American idea of democracy considers essential.

While the concept of unanimity provides the ideal which should be pursued in all forms of public activity, the lower levels of politics have witnessed a sharpening of lines of conflict. The dominant issue has been that of language. Overall, there is the controversy over the national language, Hindi, which is particularly resented by the peoples of the south and of Bengal. Then there is the question of regional languages. In 1956, the Nehru government accepted the principle of linguistic states, and the state boundaries were largely redrawn. There was an attempt to perpetuate one bilingual state, Bombay (largely because of the special position of Bombay city), but unrest continued, and in 1960 this state was bisected into Gujarat and Maharashtra. Even this division did not end all agitation. Once the linguistic principle is accepted, it appears to let loose endless demands for bifurcation. In Punjab, Assam, and other states, the language agitation festers on, the cause of bitterness and violence.

The infrastructure of Indian politics has only recently become a field for academic study.[17] British and Indian scholars have focused their attention upon the apex of the political pyramid: Morris-Jones's book is the last major work in this tradition. A systematic study of the base has had to await the American entry into Indian political studies. The literature of American political science and sociology is much taken up with the inside and underside of politics: 'the grass-roots', and the 'smoke-filled room', are phrases which epitomise this approach. Its application to India within the last few years has initiated something of an academic revolution. The first notable American contribution was *Leadership and Political Institutions in India*, a symposium which had its origins in a seminar organised by the Modern India Project of the University of California, Berkeley.[18] The twenty-nine papers are

[17] The present writer was a pioneer in this field: see H. Tinker, *Foundations of Local Self-Government in India, Pakistan, and Burma*, London, 1954.

[18] R. L. Park and I. Tinker (eds.), *Leadership and Political Institutions in India*, Princeton, 1959.

grouped into eight sections which consider "Traditions of Leadership", "Personality and Leadership", "Political Institutions", "Political Parties", "Influence Groups", "Public Administration", "Rural Development and Administration", and "Leadership and Change in the Village". The last three sections are those which contribute most to a new understanding of Indian politics. The section on public administration includes a study of the National Planning Commission. This body—which is virtually independent of parliament—forms (in the words of the auditor general of India) 'the economic cabinet not merely for the Union but also for the states'. By means of the Five Year Plans it is able to shape a national economic, social, and political philosophy. For example, it can determine what proportion of new industry shall be allotted to public corporations and what to private enterprise. The direction of industry towards individual states is also under its control. This body has no counterpart in any western democratic country. Also in this section, the changing role of the public services in the present transition period between bureaucratic and popular rule is considered. The implications of the uneasy triangle of relationships between civil servants, the public, and the politicians are explored. The attempt to graft a system of local self-government on to India's tradition of autocracy is another aspect of political change which is examined. The following section on rural development surveys the massive Community Development programme, under which the 500,000 villages of India are gradually being associated with plans for rural reconstruction.[19] The final section on village life affords a somewhat gloomy impression of the remoteness of the village folk from the functioning of the new democracy. It becomes evident that the forces of caste and faction are nowhere declining. Rather, men are becoming more conscious of their caste-ties. The lower castes attempt to raise themselves up the social ladder not by individual effort but by joint caste action; similarly, the upper castes band together to resist the advance of these upstarts.

There is an obvious lacuna in *Leadership and Political Institutions in India*: the all-important area of states politics. This gap is filled by a work which is perhaps the most significant individual contribution to Indian studies since independence: *India, the Most*

[19] By May 1961, the Community Development Programme had reached, to some extent, 368,200 villages with a population of 203 million.

Dangerous Decades, by Selig S. Harrison.[20] The author spent three years as a journalist in South Asia. He examines, dispassionately, a problem which even today it is difficult to broach without being accused of bias: the question whether India is heading towards unification or disintegration.

Mr Harrison begins with a historical survey; he examines the geographical features which have isolated the various regions of the subcontinent, the multiplication of languages and dialects which resulted, and the regional myths and legends which have been perpetuated, making for local pride, and contempt for adjacent peoples. Next, he contrasts the English-speaking middle class, which came forward in the nineteenth century, with the emergent *petit bourgeois* 'regional élites' which resulted from the revival of regional languages and literatures, and which now dominate state politics and government. The politics of language are accompanied by the politics of caste; especially in south India. Certain local political parties have been formed on a caste and tribe basis, such as the Virashaiva Mahasabha of the Lingayats, and the Jharkand Party of the Adibasis or aboriginals of Bihar. More often, the caste lobbies take over the main parties at the state level and manipulate them in the caste interest. A striking example is found in Andhra in the caste conflict between the Kammas and Reddis: these competing castes have taken over Congress and the Communist Party for their own platforms. Mr Harrison makes a special study of communist policy in relation to regionalism, and attempts to estimate how far the communists have succeeded in exploiting language and caste, and how far misjudgement of these factors has had repercussions upon the party. He decides: 'Indian communism will not, by itself, provide a pan-Indian alternative to the Congress Party. Indian communism is a loose federation of regional units that have succeeded, where they have in fact succeeded, only on regional grounds. The pattern of failure, too, corresponds to regions in which rivals have monopolised regional patriotism. With its strength dispersed in scattered regional strongholds, Indian communism seems committed by its past to a separatist future.' (p. 178) Harrison sees the separatist movements in south India as the main potential instruments of communist strategy. He underlines the identification of the national

[20] Selig S. Harrison, *India, the Most Dangerous Decades*, Princeton, 1960.

language, Hindi, with the national party (Congress), and both with the great northern state, Uttar Pradesh. Fear of 'Hindi imperialism' is a potent force in rallying the separatists: and the Hindi speakers form only 30 per cent of India's total population. Mr Harrison is not optimistic in his assessment of the chances of the Indian Union surviving under its present form of government. He considers that centralised control is unlikely to be enforced by democratic processes; the alternative seems to be unity enforced by totalitarian rule, or democracy and decentralisation.

The role of the Communist Party in this situation is, of course, crucial. Harrison is far from accepting the usual picture of the party as an irresistible juggernaut. Will the caste system and the Hindu outlook act as solvents which will reshape communism into an Indian mould, as Hinduism has largely accepted and assimilated conquest by Islamic Central Asia and Christian Britain? Or will communism rise to power on a wave of social discontent and economic distress? A full-scale inquiry has been conducted by two American political scientists, Gene D. Overstreet and Marshal Windmiller in their opus *Communism in India*.[21] They first trace the historical development of Indian communism before independence. Far from being the monolithic proletarian movement which is so frequently depicted, the nascent CPI was a slender, scattered coterie of intellectuals, drawing its nourishment entirely from abroad and without 'grass-roots'. M. N. Roy, its leader, was an émigré, and almost all directives came from the International, or from the British Communist Party.[22] Communism made its first important advance during the years 1942–5, when the Congress was inactive. The communists came out in support of the British government in the 'People's War', and under the cloak of official toleration increased their membership from 5,000 in 1942 to 53,000 in 1945. After independence, the twists and turns of policy and practice became even more tortuous. Russian influence remained paramount, and the policy of Mao Tse-tung was at first repudiated, and then belatedly accepted. The policy of insurrection or guerrilla war was

[21] Gene D. Overstreet and Marshal Windmiller, *Communism in India*, Berkeley, 1959.

[22] The 'imperialist' relationship of French, Dutch, and British communists with their comrades in their countries' own colonies is one of the curiosities of communist technique.

in turn discarded for constitutional methods. These reversals were accompanied by the familiar party purges and public self-criticism. Russian policy, which at one time labelled Nehru as a 'running dog' of imperialism, veered to the adulation of Nehru, the statesman of world peace: this did not help the CPI, but their greatest shock came with the Chinese occupation of Tibet and the later incursions over the Sino-Indian border. Communist successes have owed much less to successful propaganda and organisation on an all-India basis than to the exploitation of local discontents. The authors describe how the communist policy of a 'multi-national' India emerged. As early as 1940, the communists endorsed the Muslim League's demand for Pakistan, and in 1942 the existence of sixteen 'nations' (i.e. language groups) in India was recognised. By 1950, the CPI had decided to oppose the introduction of Hindi as the national language, and at every opportunity supported the regional languages. Overstreet and Windmiller brought their study to an end just as the communist government in Kerala was taking office. They were not, therefore, able to analyse this most interesting sector of the struggle. They were only able to speculate on the possibility of the party discarding the dogma which (in their view) has restricted progress like a strait-jacket. They end up with this observation on the CPI: 'Up to now, its nature has been more communist than Indian. But it has shown some flexibility and adaptability—especially in the realm of tactics. Should it become even a little more Indian, it will be truly a force to be reckoned with.'

Among recent Indian writings upon politics and government, the work of Dr A. R. Desai of the Department of Sociology in the University of Bombay deserves attention. His ideas are placed firmly in a conceptual framework; he sees the rise of nationalism as a phenomenon in causal relationship to economic and social forces. In his attempt to create a framework for Indian political studies, it is unfortunate that Dr Desai employs a crude Marxian interpretation of history. He is very far from being a communist, but like so many Asian intellectuals his thought is confined within Marxian dialectical materialism. We find him arguing in his best known book, *Social Background of Indian Nationalism*,[23] that Indian nationalism did not grow out of the influence of western education, but was 'the

[23] Dr A. R. Desai, *Social Background of Indian Nationalism*, Bombay, 3rd ed., 1959.

outcome of the new social material conditions created ... as a result of the British conquest. ... The movement arose out of the conflict of British and Indian interests in the economic and other spheres.' (p. 145) His Marxian basis leads him to introduce into his account of the rise of new classes in India during and after the nineteenth century a section on 'peasant movements' and 'peasant revolts'. Now, there is no feature of Indian life more striking than the peasants' immobility; call it apathy or call it resignation. Perhaps the most horrifying feature of the great Bengal famine of 1943 was the patient acceptance with which the peasants met starvation, knowing that within the village grain shop lay sacks of foodgrains. It is this attitude of acquiescence which forms the greatest barrier to the successful promotion of the Community Development schemes for village self-help. It is this same acquiescence which stultifies the efforts of communist workers to stimulate revolutionary fervour. Yet Desai sees the peasants as a dynamic force. Looking at the effect of social and economic change on group loyalties, he discerns the emergence of what he calls a 'national bourgeoisie' and a 'national proletariat'. While it is certain that local isolation has been broken down by improved communications and other changes, we have seen that the growth of an all-India consciousness has been restricted to the Anglicised upper middle class. Desai's concentration upon economic motivation leads him to discern 'a peculiarity of the Indian nationalist movement' in that the bourgeoisie 'exhibited compromising tendencies and desired for [sic] a settlement with the ruling imperialism. This was due to the fact that the Indian bourgeoisie was interlocked with reactionary landlord and moneylending classes in the country, was dependent, due to its economic weakness, on the British finance capital and was afraid of the growing dimension of the mass movement interpreting it as a danger to its own interest. ... Such a spectacle unfolded the perspective of the Indian nationalist movement culminating in a non-bourgeois victory of the national forces and of a path of socialist development in the post-independence phase.' (pp. 356–7) It is clear that, at the time he wrote these words, Desai expected this victory to follow shortly. However, his views were somewhat modified in a sequel, *Recent Trends in Indian Nationalism*.[24] Again, the central

[24] Dr A. R. Desai, *Recent Trends in Indian Nationalism*, Bombay, 1960.

theme can be summarised in one passage: 'Only socialism can end the present crisis of the Indian society. It alone can ... advance the Indian people on the road of a still higher socialist material and cultural existence.' (p. 138) Desai explains the enigma of the Congress capitulation to the Partition of India in the terms of the 'timid and compromising' character of Indian capitalism: 'Afraid of the masses, it dared not organise revolutionary mass movements.' (p. 53) Desai accuses the Congress of lacking any original thinking about forms of government; he argues that at all periods the bourgeois Congress leaders have been content to imitate British political models. India today is a capitalist country, he insists; and the complex apparatus of planning, and the public ownership of industry, power resources, etc., is merely a means of buttressing capitalism; 'the state's active participation in the national economy has become indispensable for preserving the capitalist system in the present epoch of monopoly capitalism'. (p. 79) In the field of agriculture, Desai finds that capitalist interests are again paramount. The so-called abolition of *zamindari* (landlordism) has only led to the creation of a class of substantial farmers: 'So far as the poor and middle peasantry are concerned, the working out of the agrarian policy together with other programmes has ... even resulted in the further deterioration of [their] conditions.' (pp. 95–6) All these arguments deserve our earnest consideration, particularly concerning agriculture. We may accept the good intentions of the Congress governments in abolishing *zamindari*, but the main consequence is the further depression of the lower classes, which Desai describes.

If the main politico-economic argument is identical with that in the earlier book, Desai's views on the growth of national feeling have been modified. In his definition of nationality, Desai falls back on the accepted communist position: nationality is equated with the regional language groups. 'Each nationality area' is a linguistic region; of a higher, Indian nationalism he has nothing to say.

In his conclusion, Dr Desai states: 'Much as we dislike to make such a prognosis, the actual process of development (or decline) of the Indian society from year to year unfolds such a gloomy prospect. Under capitalism it is not possible to liquidate mass poverty, mass unemployment, mass illiteracy and mass ignorance.' (p. 137) A great many people have been working to contravert this prediction.

The accent is usually placed upon democracy, rather than capitalism, as the cause which is at stake. India is a democracy: the 'shop window' of democracy in Asia, publicists say. But India is also miserably poor: income per capita today is only Rs. 280 (US $60) per annum. Unless India can raise the standard of living of the great mass of the poor, then they will abandon their faith in democracy. But can India achieve a significant increase in national income by the methods of a free society? Can a peasant, agricultural population develop better methods of production voluntarily—by encouragement and exhortation—or is the communist technique of mass compulsion and direction the only way to achieve the 'Great Leap Forward'? In this predicament, should not the wealthy nations of the West provide economic aid to assist the Indian economy to reach the point of 'take-off into self-sustained growth'?[25] The argument that democracy in Asia can become well-established only if it is seen to be capable of 'delivering the goods' in material terms is one that has distinguished advocates: among them the bankers' mission which visited India in 1960—Sir Oliver Franks, Mr Allan Sproul, and Dr Hermann Abs. The present writer is not prepared to accept all the implications of this materialist argument, which appears to be merely the capitalist counterpart to the promises of communism. The peoples of Asia are today searching for something more than full stomachs. At the same time, one cannot deny that democracy and an empty stomach are not enough. Nehru had sensed all this: he said: 'Political freedom under economic pressure is very limited freedom ... how can creativeness come out of hunger and poverty, even though a man has got a vote? ... I believe in democracy and democratic institutions. ... But again, in the final analysis, you come back not to political terms, not to economic terms, but to some human terms or, if you like, spiritual terms. We want to produce a good life, a good individual.'[26]

An author whose ideas are much in accord with these beliefs, and who has become increasingly the champion of economic aid to underdeveloped countries as a means of upholding the 'free world'

[25] The concept of the 'take-off into self-sustained growth' is the creation of Professor W. W. Rostow, and his theory has had a great influence on the Second Five Year Plan in India.

[26] See Jawaharlal Nehru, *Future of Asian Democracy*, New Delhi, 1959, pp. 5–8.

is Barbara Ward. Her views are well expressed in a number of books; the most relevant to this study being *India and the West*.[27]

The book is divided into three parts. The first, called "The Revolution of Economic Growth", traces the changes which led to the Industrial Revolution in the West, and the subsequent impact of the West upon world patterns of trade and production. The second part is somewhat inexactly called "The Indian Plans". Three chapters are devoted to a survey of the transformation of India under British rule. The author characterises British policy and practice as *laisser faire*; this is a widely-accepted proposition, but it does not represent the facts. The creation of a system of communications (the essential prerequisite for 'take-off') was the work of the British government. First, trunk roads were driven across the subcontinent; then came the railways, mainly financed by public loans and grants, and operated under public control. The legacy which was handed on to independent India is thus described in the First Five Year Plan: 'The Indian railway system is the largest nationalised undertaking in the country. It is one of the few railway systems in the world with a net earning power adequate to meet all fixed charges and provide substantial sums for development and reserves.' The second great economic asset created by government initiative was the massive irrigation system which dwarfs such rivals as the Tennessee Valley Authority or the canals of Egypt. Over twenty-five million acres of arid semi-desert were brought into fruitful cultivation. These schemes brought prosperity and higher living standards to some provinces (such as Punjab), but overall there was no great improvement. The rise in production was largely absorbed by the swelling population: between 1881 and 1931, the population rose from 248 million to 338 million.

If earlier methods did little more than maintain an equilibrium between rising population and production, can the planned expansion of the present day do better? In her next three chapters, the author provides a concise account of the genesis of Indian planning and its first results. Like most observers she is impressed by achievements in industry, but dismayed by the record of agriculture: still the occupation of three-quarters of India. She puts her finger on one vital cause; agriculture is still associated with backwardness; industry and commerce with progress, in the minds of every kind of

[27] Barbara Ward, *India and the West*, London and New York, 1961.

Indian. The lively village lad, the college student, the civil servant, the politician: all want to turn their backs on the village, once described by Dr Ambedkar, the untouchables' leader, as 'a sink of localism, a den of ignorance, narrow-mindedness, and communalism'. So long as this attitude prevails, it is hard to see how any radical change can take place in the village or in peasant agriculture. Is the only solution the rise of a class of *kulak* farmers, with the inevitable further depression of the smaller peasantry? To these questions, Miss Ward does not attempt to supply answers. She returns to the larger problems of planning and capital investment. Looking at the Third Plan, she estimates that India needs for it about £5,500 million in resources to be raised outside the ordinary budget. The last part of the book, "Challenge to the West", is concerned to show why these millions should be provided out of foreign aid. It is the duty of Britain and other western nations which (as it were) launched countries like India into the modern world to make certain that they are properly equipped for their voyage. Readers are unlikely to deny the appeal which Miss Ward makes in the name of humanity and Christian justice. Economic aid should certainly be made available on a scale which will contribute to a measurable increase in standards of living in India and similar countries struggling on the edge of survival. But it is naïve to imagine that foreign aid, however generous, is the solution to the problem. The fundamental problem is that of change within Indian society. We have, in this survey, taken note of some of the forces which must be dissolved if Indian society is to become really dynamic: such forces as regional and linguistic particularism, caste and class obscurantism. These are problems which no external influence can resolve.

It is so generally assumed that the future of India depends upon the internal responses to the political experiment of democracy, and the economic experiment of planning and pressurised industrialisation, that we are apt to forget that the course of events may be shattered by pressures from outside India. The uneasy relationship with Pakistan has had recurrent internal consequences; but this external threat has been totally eclipsed by the enigma of China's intentions along her southern border.

Diplomatic relations oscillated from pole to pole between the years 1954 and 1959. In April 1954, a Sino-Indian treaty on Tibet was negotiated. This included a statement of the Five Principles of Peaceful Co-Existence, sometimes called *pancha shila*. Under this treaty, India acknowledged Chinese sovereignty over Tibet, and the special position which British India had acquired in southern Tibet came to an end. The flight of the Dalai Lama and thousands of his countrymen over the Indian border in March 1959 put a severe strain on the co-existence spirit. It became clear that China was becoming more active in the border area. Relations reached boiling point with a Chinese attack on an Indian frontier post at Longju in August 1959, followed in October by the ambush of a border patrol in Ladakh or 'Little Tibet' in which nine Indians were killed and ten taken prisoner. Since this time, the cold war has held the Himalayan borderlands in its icy grip. Is China reasserting what she takes to be her historic rights in an area from which China claims to have received periodical 'tribute' in the past? Or is China eroding India's borderlands as the first stage in a career of conquest? One writer who is convinced that 'Han imperialism' is on the march is Frank Moraes, the outspoken editor of the *Express* group of newspapers in India. *The Revolt in Tibet* is a vigorous account of the Chinese invasion of Tibet which,[28] he believes, is the prelude to the Chinese penetration of South-East Asia and the overthrow of democratic government in India. Even if these fears are unduly alarmist, if the Indian government is compelled to devote an even larger proportion of the meagre national resources to defence, and to clamp down on internal opposition for fear of subversion, then the prospects for democracy and for social welfare and development are shadowy indeed.

It will not have escaped the reader that all the books cited in this article are in the English language (though their authors belong to several nationalities). In truth, within the field of Indian nationalism, the choice of works in other European languages is small. There are some general studies of independent India in French and German,[29] but the particular contribution of scholars of continental Europe to Indian studies has been in the field of anthropology, philosophy, and religion. As the author of a delightful introductory essay wittily observes: 'Par quelle fatalité ne parle-t-on plus de

[28] Frank Moraes, *The Revolt in Tibet*, New York, 1960.
[29] For example, Father Yvon, *Le drame de l'Indépendance Indienne*, Paris, 1952; Heinrich Gutersohn, *Indien, eine Nation im Werden*, Berne, 1953.

l'Inde, en France et ailleurs, depuis quelques années, que les yeux levés au ciel?'[30] There is a great need for students of politics and economics from continental Europe to turn their attention to India, both in the spheres of academic and of practical assistance.

It is the central thesis of this survey that the most significant development in India since independence is the rise of regional, linguistic nationalism, at odds with the westernised, all-India nationalism which formerly occupied the political stage; further, that the most significant academic development has been the growth of studies of the infrastructure of Indian politics and society.

This trend may be illustrated by reference to two recent major efforts to examine the politics of individual states: one work is by a political scientist, descending from the observation of nationwide, ideological politics into the arena of the politics of language and caste; the other work demonstrates a physical anthropologist raising his sights from the 'little society' of the village to a wider environment. Myron Weiner's *The Politics of Scarcity* (Chicago, 1962) has the sub-title, *Public Pressure and Political Response in India*, but its significance mainly emerges from the regional context of the study. Weiner conducted his researches for this work in West Bengal, an area of peculiar political sensitivity and volatility. He examines the political techniques of different types of pressure group: caste associations, trade unions, university students, business and industry, among others. His inquiry leads him to consider the role of physical violence in modern India. He demonstrates that these pressures are almost entirely opposed to the centralised, planned, policy of the government of India, and indicates that in future the clash of interest is likely to be intensified.

F. G. Bailey has already minutely examined the politics of the tribal fringe of rural India in *Caste and the Economic Frontier* (Manchester, 1957) and other works. In *Politics and Social Change; Orissa in 1959* (Berkeley, 1963) Bailey considers a cross-section of state politics, from village level, through the constituency, to the State Assembly and the state party organisations. By contrast to West Bengal, Orissa remains a mainly static society, dominated by a traditional status hierarchy. Bailey begins in the village, where politics is involved with family and caste relationships, inter-group disputes and feuds, and the deals and manœuvres which result from

[30] Madeleine Biardeau, *Inde*, Bourges, 1958, p. 5.

37367

this situation. Because this is the overall atmosphere of village politics, perhaps Bailey tends to see state politics in the same terms, with 'fixing' as the main purpose of all politicians. His approach is remarkably similar to that of Namier in his investigation of the network of interests in eighteenth-century England: except that a political system based upon universal suffrage has even more extensive interests to accommodate.

The principal studies of state politics yet to appear have been produced by American and British scholars. There is a need for indigenous academic studies of the infrastructure of Indian politics. To urge this is not to neglect the importance of original thinking about the means whereby the vision of Indian unity may be realised. If it is true to suggest that India is a civilisation rather than a country, then there is a special Indian dilemma in the reconciliation of sometimes divergent regional movements with all-India aspirations. China appears to have solved much the same problem of regionalism through a communist version of the Confucian concept of all members of the nation as a family. Can India evolve a similar synthesis of the traditional and modern, founded in the democratic outlook?

At last the country is confronting the crisis awaited so long with dread: an India without Nehru. The first phase seems to indicate that fears may have been exaggerated. The process whereby Lal Bahadur Shastri was 'evolved' as prime minister was an impressive demonstration of how local Congress leaders in the various states had learnt to co-ordinate and combine for a national purpose. Yet the subsequent unhappy handling of the long-postponed replacement of English by Hindi at the all-India level, and the violent demonstrations of hostility to Hindi in the Dravidian south, showed how much deep-felt loyalty 'linguism' (that is, regional, linguistic nationalism) can generate and sustain. A more decentralised political system seems inevitable, if a unified India is to survive.

A nation in making, or breaking? So many questions remain unanswered. An approach still has to be worked out to cope with China's aggressive border policy: an approach not founded in either vacillation or in panic militarisation. The problem almost defies solution. But India has survived thousands of years of internal and external pressures. India will endure.

6

The Name and Nature of Foreign Aid

A LMOST unconsciously, diplomacy and international relations have acquired a new and powerful component: foreign economic aid. From the days of Britain's subsidies to her Continental allies against Napoleon, wartime aid has been an element in policy. Peacetime aid was born, virtually, with the Marshall Plan, in the late 1940s. It has since come to stay as a permanent feature of foreign policy. It is time that its significance was studied on a level other than that of day-to-day requirements. This paper makes no attempt to comment on aid in its strictly economic aspects. It does attempt to discuss the psychology of aid, some problems of administration, the kind of service that is desirable, and the long-term effects that aid may help to produce in the world. Throughout, emphasis is placed upon posing questions rather than on providing solutions, which the writer cannot make any pretence of supplying.

Very little attention has been paid to the psychological stresses which surround the provision of aid in Asia.[1] The newly independent nations still find it difficult to take for granted that they are free, that European domination has gone for ever. An invisible Union Jack still floats over the Red Fort at Delhi. Any suspicion that vestiges of colonialism remain, in the economic or even the cultural sphere, can immediately arouse a wave of feeling in political

[1] A notable assessment was made in a *Times* leader, "Tomorrow's Aid", cf. *The Times*, July 19, 1956; cf. also "Combating the Russian Threat in Asia", *The Times*, June 27, 1956.

and official circles, and to a lesser extent among the general public. Yet, at a deeper level, there remains a need for a substitute for the now departed imperial authority. A hundred years of foreign rule does not equip a people for assuming all the heavy burdens of statehood and national development. The term 'slave mentality' which many Asians invoke to describe their state of mind under western dominance may be crude; but it is clear that when another nation withholds responsibility for all decisions of policy—foreign relations, defence, even execution of most of the important details of routine administration—this does not contribute to the promotion of a spirit of self-reliance.[2] 'I cannot take the responsibility...'—that phrase will awake echoes in the memories of former administrators. And so, while independence was demanded and fought for by Asian leaders, its attainment makes a process of adjustment necessary. Learning to assume responsibility comes automatically only to the most outstanding of the new nations' statesmen and senior officials. There is a longing for some substitute for the former imperial umbrella: yet this longing is repudiated, despised, if ever it enters into the levels of conscious thought.

Aid has a straightforward job to do in providing technicians and equipment which are scarce in underdeveloped countries, but nowhere is its application straightforward—always there are tensions. If it appears to be a cloak for the return of political control or influence in however indirect form, then its benefits will be submerged by emotional cross-currents. So much of American aid has been suspect because it is believed that the United States wishes the recipient to identify himself unquestioningly with American foreign policy. The nomenclature of some American programmes, such as the Mutual Security Administration, has appeared to emphasise this commitment. Therefore, assistance available under the various UN agencies, or even under the Colombo Plan, is more acceptable, because it does not suffer from this stigma of identification with foreign policy. The endless disclaimers which are put out by the apologists of certain governments about American aid only being accepted 'without strings' underline these preoccupations. Indeed, in

[2] For a discussion of 'the slave mentality', see chapters by the present writer, "The Impact of Western Democracy on Asia" and "Democratic Institutions in India and China", in W. Burmeister (ed.), *Democratic Institutions in the World Today*, London and New York, 1958.

some Asian countries most heavily in receipt of American aid, it has become a matter of routine to display hostility to the United States in the press and elsewhere in order to demonstrate spiritual independence. The aid programme has backfired upon the donor in unrequited ill will.

The foreign expert also has an unenviable part to play in providing an unacknowledged substitute for the imperial decision-taker of a former day. All the new states have subscribed to the belief that economic development must proceed on the basis of state planning. Probably only in India has the actual drafting of the framework of the plan been the work of nationals. In half a dozen other lands, from Persia to the Philippines, the blueprint has been drawn by foreign experts, mainly Americans. In these circumstances, responsibility for setting up the target (and hence, to a great extent, for hitting it) does not fall squarely upon the shoulders of the national leaders. Moreover, foreign experts have been utilised to evade responsibility for failures in specific cases. Let us suppose that a newly nationalised enterprise reveals, after the first few years, certain grave defects which reflect upon the politicians and officials in charge. One solution to this embarrassment is to call in foreign experts to inquire and report. This clearly demonstrates that the government is doing something constructive. The experts investigate, make recommendations, and fly away. The government is now free to carry out the experts' proposals, or to shelve them, as it wishes. Honour is satisfied. It would be quite false to describe such a technique as general, or even perhaps predominant; but the foreign expert is no stranger to the role of stalking-horse or scapegoat in Asia today.

Another legacy from the colonial period is the conviction that the poverty of Asia is the consequence of exploitation by the West. Hence the belief, shared by many, that the West owes a debt to Asia which can only be repaid by copious material assistance today. The West is 'richer by Asia': a reciprocal movement is now overdue. Most countries have come to regard foreign aid as something which should be provided as an automatic service, as water is drawn from a tap. The availability of aid is taken for granted, and the solution for every financial crisis is sought in additional aid.[3] These demands,

[3] Cf. the writer's analysis of the impact of aid on one country; see *The Union of Burma*, London and New York, 3rd ed., 1961, pp. 97–125. One statement, 'American aid was received without sense of obligation' in

ever growing in volume, have been met to a large extent; and mainly by the United States. As aid has increased, upon consciousness of being in debt has been piled the frustrating belief that this indebtedness must continue indefinitely. The goal of prosperity seems to be as distant as ever. Aid on the medical front may even have worsened things; in part owing to elimination of disease, the population is increasing faster than the resources in many lands. Aid from the West seems to offer no short-term solutions; perhaps communist aid has some magic formula that will ensure success? The conducted tours of the USSR which are so lavishly arranged for Asians of any standing seem to provide corroboration. Communist aid, therefore, is invited; but western aid goes on, despite its tarnish, because Asia just cannot do without it.

These are some of the irrational elements which infuse the Asian attitude to aid. On the western side also there are illusions or delusions. Any belief that the tendering of assistance should be conditional on taking sides with the donor in the cold war has long been discarded from the thinking of the civil servants and technicians who operate the programmes. But it has not vanished from the minds of western politicians and publicists. Somewhat illogically, those who imagine that the provision of aid should be conditional on taking sides against world communism frequently expect the recipient to exhibit expressions of gratitude also. But if a price is demanded, then gratitude has no place in the transaction: economic aid is exchanged for a military understanding. Another illusion which is more widely shared is that the provision of technical aid is an automatic, self-adjusting process. Ceylon requires an expert on chicken-rearing, and (let us suppose) Australia is willing to supply one: hey presto, the problem is solved. But the chicken expert must first turn himself into an expert on natural conditions in Ceylon before his prior expertise will be of the slightest value. Neglect of this simple precaution has ruined more aid ventures than any other factor. Another western illusion, not far removed from the above, is

Burma (p. 124), was criticised by a Burmese scholar who suggested that, under Buddhism, acceptance of aid piled up an enormous spiritual debt of gratitude, quite incommensurate with the actual material value of the aid, which in certain aspects (the instance of a dredger is often cited) was defective. So the material aid was not appreciated and the incurrence of a debt of gratitude was resented.

that aid is indirectly a vehicle for the transmission of a 'way of life'. Any measure that seeks to impose a western pattern on an Asian situation will be both unsuccessful and harmful. If a foreign planner attempts to transpose the national dynamic of his western country into a plan for Asia, then the subsequent failure will have far-reaching consequences. A good expert is, of course, a good ambassador for his own country: but he should remember that the ambassador's function is not the transformation of the country of his appointment into the likeness of his native land.

One effect of national feeling creeping into aid has been an unspoken but unmistakable tone of antagonism between some British and some American experts and advisers. Some Englishmen (by no means of the old régime only) find it hard to accept the advent of Americans into southern Asia, which is still regarded as 'our' area. This resentment is expressed in criticism of American experts in the field as brash, uninformed, and doctrinaire. Some Americans, in the 'anti-colonial' tradition, arrive in Asia with a bias against most things connected with the colonial period. In advising on future developments, they find it necessary to reject or overthrow the solutions propounded by British officials in former days. As the American experts outnumber the British overwhelmingly, their influence is quantitatively much greater. There is no virtue in keeping to old ways merely because people understand them; but equally there is no infallible virtue in change.

Western aid to Asia since the war has yielded a crop thick with thorns: frustrations in the actual operation of the programmes, expensive lack of success in many sectors, the palpable absence of improved relations. Many have asked, is it worth it? Mr George Kennan spoke for a growing body of opinion in a Reith Lecture when he called for a much more discriminating implementation of aid.[4] Failures must, however, be treated as a challenge. Vast and sometimes wasteful expenditure, repercussions in terms of international ill will, and unpredictability in results are accepted by the United States and Britain as part of the price to be paid in the development of nuclear and space weapons. These are accorded the highest priority as the great deterrent against a victory by Soviet communism through war, though it appears decreasingly likely that

[4] George F. Kennan, *Russia, The Atom, and the West: The BBC Reith Lectures, 1957*, London and New York, 1958.

a world war forms part of communist strategy. The stakes in the political and economic struggle between the free society and totalitarianism are equally high. In this struggle, aid is the West's only 'deterrent'. It should be accorded a priority in expenditure and planning equal to, or perhaps taking precedence over, nuclear and missile development. The communist advance by 'constitutional' means is already proceeding, and communist parliamentary groups have achieved positive successes in parts of Asia—successes that may be repeated in Africa and South America. Against these Fabian tactics of communism the West can do little directly. The leadership of democratic statesmen in South and South-East Asia is the only barrier. Unless the economic planning of the democratic governments in the area manifestly yields results in terms of general economic betterment, it is difficult to take an optimistic view of the future.

This analysis is a deliberate over-simplification of the purpose of aid in Asia, but probably only in such terms can its expansion be made acceptable to the western statesmen and electorates.

Western aid must be made to succeed on two levels. First, in the purely material sense. If x number of engineers, y quantity of equipment, and z financial contribution is put into a scheme, the result should at least be equivalent to $x + y + z$. Up till now this has seldom been the case. Aid must also succeed in the deeper sense of helping to promote Asian confidence, confidence among the ordinary people; in helping Asians to liberate themselves from the shackles of the past, and in creating a healthier relationship between the ex-imperial powers and the anti-colonial Afro-Asian nations. It may be fruitful in this brief review to concentrate upon two topics: the form in which aid is deployed and the problem of personnel.

Aid appears to be most objectionable, emotionally, when it is proffered by a large, wealthy donor-nation to a small, poor recipient. When the operation is channelled through a regional organisation, such as the Colombo Plan, much of the emotion evaporates. The consultative machinery of the Plan, and the fact that its secretariat is international, help to promote a spirit of co-operation. Moreover, a country may be both a contributor and a recipient: India, as well as receiving aid, has made financial contributions to Burma under the Plan. The more that a 'donor-debtor' relationship can be replaced by a spirit of co-operation, the better. Ideally, perhaps, all aid should be handed over to United Nations agencies. But the UN has now accumulated a vast bureaucracy, and its officials have become very like the plutocrats of the aid world. This means that UN aid is expensive. The underdeveloped nations are required to contribute a considerable part of the costs of the experts posted to them; this part will represent a sum considerably higher than the salary of a comparable national expert. Then, if UN aid is to be available on a much larger scale, those countries providing the bulk of the contributions would wish to have some control over their commitments. In 1957 the UNESCO budget was doubled, without prior warning, as the result of a snap proposal by certain members. The major contributors could only protest and pay. (The undoubted achievements of UN agencies, such as UNICEF, in many distressing situations should not exempt the activities of these organisations from examination and comment.)

The process of procuring aid frequently needs to be less rigid. 'Help given promptly is help twice given': this is true not only of individuals. Often, assistance will be required on a long-term basis in accordance with long-term planning. But some needs arise unexpectedly, a need for a man or a machine in a particular place at a particular time. The response is often too tardy to meet such a need. The principal of a college in Swat, in the remote north-west of Pakistan, told the writer that he badly needed an English lecturer to teach in his college. When asked whether he had considered the Colombo Plan Organisation as a possible source of supply, he wryly quoted a Persian proverb, 'While waiting for the medicine, the sick man died.' Colombo Plan officials, when told this story, stressed that delay in this kind of instance is by no means all on their side. The machinery for obtaining aid badly requires streamlining in many Asian countries. A request for a malaria expert by the health ministry of a state in the Indian Union, for example, will have to ascend through half a dozen ministries and departments before it is finally cleared to a foreign-aid body. Amongst other complications, there are those arising from the determination of many in authority to apply orthodox principles of book-keeping to aid. The delivery of United States aid is conditional on the payment by the recipient of equivalent sums into a Counterpart Fund. Although it is laid down that the Counterpart Fund shall be spent within the recipient country, its disbursement often occasions bitterness. Among the recipients, in at least one Asian Commonwealth country, the government auditors ignore the purpose of aid in their book-keeping rules. An aid-financed cement factory was erected by two other Commonwealth partners. In determining the price at which the cement was to be sold, the product was costed as if the factory had been paid for out of the recipient country's budget. The resulting high prices at which the cement was marketed brought only odium upon the two outside Commonwealth helpers.

In the present inchoate phase, there is room for aid of varying types at different levels. One of the healthy features of American aid is the activity of non-governmental agencies, the Foundations. Some of these (such as the Ford Foundation) operate on a massive scale in broad projects, although within selected fields. Others (such as the Asia Foundation) are prepared to assist with small-scale ventures. In this manner a proper infrastructure of aid is created. There is need for fresh experiment in the techniques of aid. This would have to be the subject of study, but, as a possible example, surely there could be a place for the participation of British industrial firms in some programme in which they could provide skills and technical information? A model exists, to some extent, in the 'joint ventures' which have been set up in Burma on the basis of a partnership between the Union government and British oil, mining, and other enterprises.[5] There is much talk of the intercourse between Commonwealth universities; yet at the universities of India and Pakistan today a British professor is hardly ever seen, although his presence is sought and welcomed. The flow could be resumed, if the requisite conditions were created.

While experiment and imagination are needed in evolving the best means for co-ordinating and administering aid, any improvement will only be as good as the men who come out to do the actual work: the experts. Methods of recruiting experts are roughly similar under all the western aid programmes. A man is recruited to fill a particular vacancy for a limited period, usually two years. Such a system fits American society well enough, for conditions are fluid and it is quite normal for an American professional man to move around in his career: first, he may spend a period in academic research; then in government service; a spell in business or industry; then, it may be, in politics or diplomacy; and back again into academic life. Within this scheme of things, a sojourn in an Asian

[5] See Tinker, *The Union of Burma*, pp. 114–18.

country fits quite smoothly—though the recruitment of Americans has its own problems too. The dedicated American is, unjustly, regarded as a subject for satire; but it must be acknowledged that American willingness to take up overseas posts is somewhat offset by a lack of flexibility in adapting to an Asian environment. The shock of change is hard to overcome, and a United States foreign service official has observed that an expert proceeding on an eighteen-months' assignment takes six months to adapt himself, gives six months' effective work, and then requires six months in which to reorientate for his return to America.

The British professional man, on the other hand, chooses one sphere of work at the outset, and normally remains there all his days. The late war changed the pattern for some: dons became civil servants, diplomats became parachutists; but, with the war over, the pattern was accepted again, though for some it was a new pattern. For most British professional men, therefore, it is unthinkable to throw over a settled career for the doubtful glamour of a few years overseas, with no clear prospects afterwards. And so recruitment of British experts is unsatisfactory. Those who are attracted are largely young men at the start of their careers: whereas men with experience will largely be required. If the latter are persuaded to go, it is often because of the prospect of an inflated salary and tax concessions which will permit them to save money much more rapidly than in Britain. Of course, there must be Englishmen who regard this work as a form of service, but one does not often meet them.

The confinement of the expert's contribution to one brief tour of duty is the weakest feature of almost every aid programme. An ancillary weakness is the lavish standard of living provided as an inducement to brave the 'hardships' of life in the tropics. The air-conditioning, refrigerators, canned foods, large cars, and other comforts do a great deal to mask the personal goodwill and technical know-how which the expert may bring. Is there no prospect of overcoming these drawbacks by creating conditions whereby men may make a lifetime career in service to underdeveloped countries? A Commonwealth public service has often been canvassed within recent years: this is a parallel idea.[6] Conditions would be various.

[6] Cf. Sir Charles Jeffries, "Staffing Oversea Public Services", *The Times*, June 23, 1958.

In Burma or Pakistan, it may be that there is room for service by doctors, agriculturalists, and engineers in remote, rugged areas under conditions partially reminiscent of the life of a settlement officer in the old Indian Civil Service or of a pioneer Christian missionary. In India or Ceylon the demand would probably be mainly for 'back-room' experts. But, in all cases, the expert would require to identify himself wholeheartedly with his adopted country, to spend long years getting to know its languages and peoples. He would have to be paid a fair salary, comparable to that of the ics, but, unlike the short-term expert, his life would not be cramped by the foreignness of everything. Within a few years he would cast free from the artificial, sealed-off world of the local western community, and enter into the life of Asia. The refrigerator and the air-conditioning would fall into the background, and real work would be done. Is this a mirage? Its attainment would depend completely upon the agreement of Asian politicians and officials, who may well discern more disadvantages than advantages in such a service. Yet, even if the idea is impracticable, the present system certainly demands drastic revision.

The manners of some other contenders in the aid tournament should be glanced at. Technicians working on Soviet projects appear to be drafted to India or Burma without regard to personal considerations. On the job, they and their families live in communal messes, as much withdrawn from the Asia around them as the imperial Englishman was alleged to be. The austerity of their conditions may impress, but in the realm of human association little is achieved. The Japanese technician is once again a familiar figure in South-East Asia. Along with his bowl of rice, simple living conditions, and modest salary he combines efficient and well-adjusted work. He is a welcome reminder that Asia can bring off an industrial revolution based not on natural wealth but on inventiveness. Perhaps the most sympathetic figure among these rival experts is the Israeli. Sunburnt, stripped for action, he too comes from a poor land which is making itself richer by sweat and ingenuity. Many in Asia and Africa would prefer to go into partnership with Israel, whose problems are more nearly related, and who therefore sees solutions in more realistic terms. But Israel's ability to assist other nations is obviously limited.

Britain is perhaps best qualified to promote assistance in the field of training and research. Britain was the pioneer in exporting to the world not only plant and machines but services and techniques, from the early nineteenth century onwards. Britain's capacity to provide aid is limited by many factors, including her obligations as banker to the sterling area. Therefore, Britain's contribution must not be thrown about in penny packets, but concentrated where it will produce the maximum effect. Many considerations suggest that Britain should concentrate the bulk of her activities within one country—India. Most Asian nations are prevented from utilising foreign aid fully by a lack of potential 'managers' and persons educationally fitted to adapt themselves to new techniques. In these respects, India is better off than most. There is one valuable facility which Britain could consider extending at once. Because of foreign exchange difficulties, the number of young Indians coming to this country for further education and training has been severely restricted. Britain could help. Moreover, this aspect of aid, the training of Asians abroad, probably yields the biggest dividends in greater national efficiency and produces the minimum of 'side reactions' in unexpected emotion.

Why concentrate upon India? In part because of the historical ties which the past has bequeathed in the shape of common institutions and ideas, but much more because of India's importance in the future. India, along with China, is likely to be a world leader in the twenty-first century. Is this an essay in divination? Not entirely. Modern history appears to demonstrate that, in the long run, numbers are the deciding factor. Power goes with numbers. Power is related to other factors, such as wealth, organisation, national unity. The advance of Russia to primacy in Europe was delayed by 150 years. Since the eighteenth century Russia has been the most populous nation in Europe, yet from 1772 to 1917 Russian attempts at European domination were checked. However, by 1957, the year of the sputnik, Russia dominated not Europe only but a wide arc throughout the world. It may be unwise to make direct comparison between Russia, and India and China. Besides a vast population Russia possessed empty lands into which she could expand, and vast natural resources for exploitation. India and China do not have these advantages. But the 600 million people of China and the 380 million of India cannot be ignored; sooner rather than later these numbers will be felt. Unless there is an unforeseen transformation of Chinese society, that country will stand forth as the protagonist of communism. But an India in which parliamentary government and democracy are cherished would provide a stabilising influence in Asia that would help to strengthen democracy throughout the world.

This theme verges upon speculation. But perhaps it is permissible occasionally to attempt to discern the shape of distant events; shaping them, to the limited extent that we may, in advance. Foreign aid does not, perhaps, demand the same urgent reflection as the hydrogen bomb; yet, in the long run, it may prove equally far-reaching in its consequences.

7

Broken-backed States

THE cycle of violence in East Africa following independence first of all attracted our attention as an encounter between African mutineers and their British officers and the British Army—as a kitchen-sink Sepoy Revolt, 1857 in 1964 without the heroism. If one penetrates beyond the transient noisy alarums, what are the likely repercussions in government and society which this instability implies? Both in East and West Africa, the post-colonial epilogue now looks like a twilight time before the dark. Ghana embarked upon independence with some preparation and with a certain political finesse; yet within six years the régime has degenerated into a grim dictatorship. Ghana may be considered as almost the last of the 'prepared' new states, which began with India and the Philippines and ended with Malaya and Nigeria. East Africa has gained independence without preparation. In Uganda, for example, the whole process of transforming an imperial benevolent despotism into a free democracy was compressed into eighteen months. Ministers, senior civil servants, the paraphernalia of parliament, all had to be evolved out of almost nothing within that time. Not surprisingly, these houses built upon the sand have begun to crumble as soon as the first tides of disorder washed at their doors. Tanganyika and Uganda enjoyed a bare twelve months of parliamentary government before the military mutineers challenged the political leaders. Zanzibar's 'independence' lasted five weeks before dissolving into an anarchy in which the corner-boys suddenly emerged as the field-marshals and generals of imaginary forces. What will be the outcome?

Most observers see three alternatives: a communist state, a personal, rabble-rousing despotism dominated by a mob magician (a Sukarno or Nkrumah) or a military dictatorship. It is assumed that in each of these cases the régime will be tightly centralised, with power controlled by a small élite. In the opinion of the present writer, another alternative exists: the broken-backed state. Despite the massive intervention of the United Nations, the broken-backed state persists in the former Belgian Congo, and will probably provide the pattern in East Africa as well as in other areas. Let us, therefore, examine this form of quasi-government which is likely to become familiar in the coming years.

If the military writers have no further use for the broken-back metaphor, it can prove eminently useful to students of politics in the new states. At one stage, the nuclear strategists apprehended that a future war would commence by a series of atomic explosions which would destroy centres of government, the main industries, sources of power, the main lines of communication, and the capability of military forces to operate as continental armies. It was conceived that there would follow 'broken-backed warfare', in which military and guerrilla forces would continue the fighting. Military opinion now appears to calculate that the nuclear holocaust could be so all-destroying that even broken-backed warfare would not be possible.

In the states which won their independence after passing through a phase of preparation, the 'freedom struggle' was an experience which might be compared to conventional warfare. But the experiences of the unprepared states is much more like the sudden and unexpected cataclysm of a nuclear bombardment. Order is replaced by chaos.

Even the prepared new states have found difficulty in maintaining the twin propositions of freedom and order. What have been the main 'controls' in these states? First, there is the existence of a large enough westernised responsible middle class to preserve a respect for representative government. Among the new states, only India, Malaya, and the Philippines have preserved this control intact, though Ceylon, Pakistan, and Nigeria have managed to keep the essence of the parliamentary spirit alive. The next control is the establishment of a professional, trained civil service and army. This corps of guardians will provide some guarantee of order though not of freedom: but only if the will to govern emerges. At present, in South Vietnam, there is a military junta, which combined to over-throw the tyranny of President Ngo Dinh Diem, whose members cannot between themselves take up the reins of supreme power; and so the driving-force of government remains uneasily suspended in Saigon between the American embassy and the high command. Occasionally, a third control is provided by the reappearance of a traditional leader. Tradition may be represented by a religious leader or by a prince or chief with a blood-royal claim upon the people's loyalty who has the ability to reclothe the appeal of tradition in a modern guise. Such a leader is Prince Norodom Sihanouk of Cambodia, who has jumped straight from a traditional into a contemporary role, mobilising a mass loyalty by his combination of princely and proletarian appeal. Finally, of course, there is the control of a communist mass party based in peasant identification with the party. This seems to be the only means of linking public feeling with an ideal, an image, where no responsible westernised middle class exists.

Let us measure up the situation in the unprepared states to ascertain how far any of these controls might operate. First, the westernised African middle class is minute, except on the West African seaboard, and there is no real commitment to representative government. Second, there are virtually no professional guardians to uphold law and order: or even to exert a counter leverage to the politicians. The Tanganyika Rifles mutineers may have had the capacity to overpower a handful of British officers on temporary secondment and to terrorise frightened Indian shopkeepers for two glorious days: they certainly do not have the capacity to unify and organise their country. Similarly, the handful of promoted clerks and overseers who constitute the new higher civil service do not have the *élan* to present a challenge to the politicians. Here and there a traditional leader may fill the political vacuum: the Kabaka of Buganda, now president of Uganda, may well emerge as much more than a figurehead. But in general the chiefs and sultans of Africa have shown no clear capacity to bid for power: like the Indian maharajas they may be numbered among the 'rulers of yesterday'.

There remains the possibility of a communist take-over bid. In the opinion of the present writer, this danger has been grossly over-rated. When one considers the potential openings which have been presented to communist mass-movements in the Near and Middle East and in East Asia, it is remarkable how little communism has advanced during the last decade. A communist guerrilla campaign needs more than a few trigger-happy corner-boys allegedly trained in Cuba to become effective. It requires a corps of dedicated, edu-cated young men, prepared to serve for no reward in the villages and on the march. China, Vietnam, and Cuba: thus far, this dedi-cation has emerged in three revolutionary situations. Let us not forget all the communist revolutions which have fizzled out.

If this analysis is valid, then the scene is set in East Africa for broken-backed government. In essence, this pattern follows the description by an American scholar of the first Chinese republic: 'A foreign office attached to domestic chaos.' The state will enjoy full international recognition and membership of the United Nations. Its ambassadors will give cocktail parties on its national day, and both the 'free world' and the communist bloc will provide aid and advice, albeit without much enthusiasm and with total absence of effect. The government may be elected or self-appointed. The ministers will promote enlightened legislation which will never be implemented. There will be a Five Year Plan, which will be studied by western postgraduate students working on development economics and by no one else. Communications between the major towns will be maintained, and about half the letters posted will be delivered (the loss of parcels will be much heavier).

Representatives of the central government will be stationed in the districts. They will sit upon the verandahs of the imposing bungalows of the old European district officers, and they will be called district officers, but their writ will not run as far as the com-pound wall. The real power in the districts will be exercised by the men of force. Some of these will be ministers, who run their own small private armies, and who levy tribute from all the local mer-chants and traders, great and small. Then there will be the under-ground or resistance leaders, who are quite frankly bandits, and who levy their tribute from the peasants as well as the townsfolk. Finally, there will be army or military police detachments, sent to protect the rural folk, and exercising their protection with a heavy hand.

The centralised state will cease to be. The simulacrum of government will continue in the capital, but within twenty miles there will be a total divorce between appearance and reality. The man with the gun will have taken over.

Those who have read *Black Mischief* by Evelyn Waugh may conclude at this point that I have drawn upon the baroque fancy of that novelist. Not so: I have drawn upon actual situations in the Union of Burma, which may claim the distinction of forming the prototype of the broken-backed régime. In Burma there were military revolts within weeks of independence. To these were added a formidable communist underground movement, and separatist tribal resistance movements. At one period the government exercised only partial control over the capital, but (thanks partly to confusion and lack of purpose among the rebels, including the communists) the government was able to fight back and to reoccupy the main towns and reopen communications. The rebellions did not end, however; they dragged on, with much of the countryside a disputed no-man's-land. General elections took place at the intervals stipulated by the constitution, and the record of the parliamentary leaders was not unimpressive.

Gradually, arguments over the 'Burmese Way to Socialism' led to a split between the government leaders. The army intervened, at first with reluctance, and power was handed back to a prime minister handsomely endorsed by popular vote. Then the army intervened again. This time the constitution was abolished, the party politicians were locked up, the press muzzled, and the Burmese Way to Socialism proclaimed via a military dictatorship. New revolts broke out; communications were sabotaged; even the military president, General Ne Win, was ambushed and shot up. The general expropriated almost all remaining foreign investment and imposed general restrictions upon native business enterprise. The plans for development simply gathered dust in the various ministries.

Most readers, if they can accept this account of a government ground to a halt, with all democratic debate extinguished, will feel shivers of Wellsian gloom at the prospect of complete collapse which this portends. Yet although in similar circumstances a western nation would experience the death of the national spirit, in Burma, despite the negation of government, life continues and is not all barren. The difference lies in the relative importance of the political, social and religious impulses in western and non-western societies. Whereas the political model forms the basic model in our Anglo-American culture, so that government provides the national backbone, in southern Asia (and I suspect in Africa also) politics is little more than a cloak, which may be assumed or discarded without too much inconvenience. The real source of strength lies in religion, in the family and the local community, in tradition, and often in magic.

If we venture into a market town in Burma today, the district officer is impotent, the network of outside communications is spasmodic at best, the hand of the military lies heavy over all. But life goes on. The brilliant festivals which mark the cycle of the year are still mounted with *brio* and gaiety around the local pagoda. Amid the chaos, religion (and magic) offers tranquillity and the means of liberation upon a non-material wavelength. The social security system which is built into the extended family still operates. A promising nephew is given lodging and assisted through college. An orphan niece or an aged aunt is given protection. A shiftless cousin is found a minor post in the office of a friend. Even the paralysing web of government regulations upon business enterprise is circumvented. A little weaving factory is set up, powered by a stuttering factory generator. Textiles—blankets, let us say—are manufactured. They are packed up in an aged lorry, and dispatched with an adventurous young man, well primed with bribery-money to get him through the many check-posts on the way. At length the blankets reach the big city and are delivered quietly to the retailer. The manufacturer, the adventurous young man, and the retailer are all related. They operate a network of family trust in which forms and files have no place. And they survive and flourish.

Where the web of government and economic life is so much more loose, and indeed more perfunctory than in our complex, highly integrated western systems, an almost complete breakdown of the national machinery does not entail a similar breakdown in local life. And so there is no dramatic national collapse: there is just broken-backed government. Very few western journalists have understood this proposition. Let us take Indonesia: bankrupt, stricken by spiralling inflation, with most of its former sources of foreign exchange (such as the rubber plantations) gone back to the jungle. For more than a decade, well-informed foreign correspondents have confidently predicted, at regular intervals, that Indonesia 'cannot last another month'. They have proved this with figures. Yet Indonesia limps along; hardly a state at all by the standards of aseptic Scandinavian social democracy; but still there, all the same.

No doubt, today, western correspondents in Dar-es-Salaam and Kampala are giving the present régimes another six months' lease of life, at most. It is far too early to write them off. Broken-backed government may seem a poor thing to those fortunate enough to live under more dynamic systems of government. But it has a quality which hard-bitten politicians rate highly: survival.

8

Race, Nationalism and Communalism in Asia

THIS brief survey of race and communalism in Asia does not cover the Near and Middle East, or Soviet Asia. In both these areas, powerful ideologies, past and present, have shaped the attitudes of their peoples upon distinctive patterns. The area remaining under consideration, eastern and southern Asia, from Japan to Pakistan, is sufficiently vast and varied to ensure that for every generality advanced below it would be easy to counter with an exception. But—to begin the generalising—within this continent, in contrast to South Africa, the races and racial attitudes are seldom sharply defined. Everywhere in southern and eastern Asia the races 'blend and blur' and (as a rule) only the recent, long-distance immigrants can be sharply differentiated. Nevertheless, there is a corpus of traditional feeling and custom regarding 'outsiders' that shapes popular attitudes and produces something akin to racialism.

First, let us attempt a broad classification of racial types in Asia. The European scholars who began to classify the peoples of southern Asia early in the nineteenth century often did not distinguish between race and language. In India, a basic distinction was drawn between the Aryan and Dravidian 'races'. Yet a south Indian Brahman speaking, for example, Kanarese (of the Dravidian group) might be descended from Indo-European stock. In South-East Asia, tribal lines have usually been drawn by ethnologists according to language or dialect, whereas some tribes are known to have adopted the language of more powerful neighbours in order to assimilate towards a desired social status or economic level. But if it is scientifically inaccurate to equate language with race, the older ethnologists were not in error in singling out language as the prime cause of unity and division. In Asia, as in Europe,[1] the members of one's own language group are in a much closer affinity than members of other language groups: as in Europe, language is the basis of nationality.[2] Race (however established biologically) is not so tangible a bond as language.

The racial diversity of Asia cannot be satisfactorily described within this chapter. The great Mongoloid family which stretches from Siberia, across eastern Asia, out into Oceania, and over the mountain barrier of north India, may be divided into many types, such as Malaysian (peopling Taiwan and most of island South-East Asia), the mixed Japanese, the southern Mongoloid, and the great Han or northern Mongoloid race, as well as others. Southern Asia has been settled successively by Negritoid, Veddoid (or Australoid), Melanesoid and Indid (Aryan). In certain cases, geographical remoteness or isolation has preserved a group in a 'pure' form as a distinct type (as in the Andamans) while caste in India has helped to perpetuate separate physical types. But even within a tribe or a caste there will be measurable variations in pigmentation, hair form, blood type or other inherited physical features. A relatively limited and isolated area such as East Bengal contains individuals exhibiting Caucasoid, Mongoloid and perhaps Melanesoid traits; but all these individuals regard themselves as Bengalis, because all speak Bengali; and because of their Islamic inheritance they have now identified themselves with the Pakistani nation. Group solidarity in Asia is much less founded upon fact (what one is, according to racial type) than upon fancy (how one thinks of oneself, in terms of language, religion and other differentials). Group solidarity has traditionally extended to a relatively small social unit, but today this is slowly giving way to an identification with the nation state—but this process has been completed only in one Asian country—Japan.

Traditionally, Asian society has been composed of communities, not individuals, and the ties of community membership have worked

[1] The English-speaking Irish are the most important exception.

[2] India forms a partial exception to this dictum: the Indian situation will be examined later.

against the individual identifying himself with the nation. In areas of ancient settlement (such as the riverine plains of north India and north China) the community has been the village: the nucleated village in the midst of its fields. Another foundation for community was kinship (often traced from remote times) in the tribe, caste or clan. Kinship ties might be coterminous with the village itself, but more often (for example, among the widely scattered Muslim tribes of western Punjab) it spread far beyond. In South-East Asia still another kind of community, the 'service group' or regiment, held sway. In upper Burma there were village communities designated as cavalry, infantry and warboatmen, while in Siam the whole population was classified into categories according to trade or service. In all these communities, there were elements, however atrophied by time, that went back to the earliest stages of the formation of human associations: the patriarchal family, common interests in land settlement and cultivation, mutual defence, interrelated economic functioning.

What of the larger loyalties? Everywhere there was allegiance to a ruler who was in some sense a protector, whether a petty hill chieftain or a semi-divine monarch, as in Japan or Hinduised South-East Asia. Frequently this ruler would perform a ritual part in the cycle of seedtime and harvest: such was the 'Royal Ploughing' in Burma, when the king by starting the ploughing of the royal paddy fields ensured an abundance in the harvest. Religion was sometimes a very positive bond, as, for example, among the Muslim puritans, the *Wahabi*, who actively and fraternally pursued their duty of creating the 'Rule of the Faithful', *dar ul Islam*. But religion was more usually a less tangible cultural link: the Buddhist pilgrim, travelling from monastery to monastery, would find in the Burmese *kyaung* and the Siamese *wat* a common matrix of learning and religion. But this did not prevent continual wars between the kings of Burma and Siam.

Speakers of a single language, as has been suggested, were co-heirs to a common cultural tradition. The Indian expression, *madari zaban*, 'mother speech', well exemplifies this family sense. How far can one talk of a sense of nationalism—in its modern application—as prevailing in traditional Asia? It has often been argued that nationalism is a product of western ideas, yet even in India, least nationalistic of Asian societies, there was a sense of *Aryavarta*, the land of the Aryans, bounded on the north by the Himalaya, home of the gods, to the west by the Indus, and to the east by the Brahmaputra. Within these bounds was the holy land of Hinduism, and six centuries of Muslim domination did not efface folk-tales of the Ramayana and Prithvi Raj. Autochthonous hill peoples, Bhils, Konds, Santals, etc. (now termed Adibasis), were outside the Hindu system. But a process of absorption began among their chiefs who often acquired Sanskritic pedigrees and emerged as Kshattriyas, or knights of the second Hindu caste. Hinduisation of tribal society at large slowly continues, as in the Kond Mahals of Orissa today. In China there was the much more intensive cultural nationalism of Confucius, defining minutely the relations between the state and the subjects. The outer, non-Han races were required to conform to the Confucian model. The process was compulsive—especially among the southern tribes—rather than assimilative as in India. In Burma, Siam, Japan, there was, among the dominant ethnic group, a definite sense of folk pride and history. By contrast, in the archipelago that now forms the Philippines and Indonesia it is difficult to find any 'national' myth that even roughly can be correlated with the political boundaries of today. Even in lands where there was a sense of country and cultural unity, the actualities of society, poor communications and local self-sufficiency served to make local life provincial and isolated.

How did traditional Asian societies regard foreigners? Much the same as in medieval Europe. In the great trading marts, along the Silk Road and other trade routes, the foreigner was accepted and his position was recognised and regulated. But unless made familiar by trade, or equally by religious pilgrimage, the foreigner was the object of suspicion and often hostility. Hostility (it is perhaps unnecessary to add) increased in direct ratio to the numbers of the foreigners. And over all was the suspicion of the outsider who might somehow bring pollution or might herald aggression. The Indian term *mleccha* denotes someone outside society, not ritually acceptable. Chinese self-sufficiency and the Chinese attitude to all foreigners as tributaries or clients is well known.[3] In South-East Asia there

[3] In nineteenth-century documents, Chinese officials referred to foreigners as *I*, which is usually given the connotation of 'barbarian' (e.g., *Nan-I*, 'southern barbarians' for the people of South-East Asia and the Europeans). But they also used the neutral expression *Wai-Kuo-Jen*

was a reciprocal attitude of arrogance. Sir Hugh Clifford describes the game 'Main China' as it was played in old Malaya. Malays would bet on the sum of money carried by a Chinese stranger, and would cut off his head to ascertain who had guessed right. 'Why cut off his head?' asked Clifford. 'Oh, it was more fun ... and he was only a Chinese.'

Among the motives for Asian aversion to foreigners that parallel the prejudices found in the West, religion and economic rivalry predominate.[4] The Chinese miner, or the Indian trader, by his industry, trade connections or technical superiority, would often outpace the indigenous Malay or Burman. In religion, the foreigner's habits were often visibly offensive. To the Hindu, with his elaborate regimen of ritual cleanliness, the Muslim or the Christian, with their laxer standards of personal hygiene, appeared dirty, even disgusting. The Muslim Malay resented the Chinese keeping pigs. On the other hand, the Buddhist Burman resented the Muslim Indian slaughtering cattle, whether for food or ritual sacrifice. Where the foreigner was a fellow-believer (like the Arab trader in a Muslim port in Sumatra or Malaya) he was much more easily fitted into society.

Race relations entered an entirely new phase with the arrival of the Europeans. As early as the fifteenth century the Portuguese were creating a new kind of racial hatred by their policy of terrorism in the name of Christ. But the main impact of the West—as expressed in policy, administration and ideas—came only in the early nineteenth century. Gradually, as the power of the West was unrolled, the most progressive Asians decided that their countries could only survive and develop in an age of western dominance if they were reformed and reinvigorated by the introduction of western ideas and techniques. In India, Ram Mohan Ray led the way with a demand for western education and for western political and civil rights; such

or 'men from abroad'. *Yang-Kuei-Tzu*, 'foreign devils', and other such epithets are used in the same way that other nations refer to 'wogs' or 'gooks', although the Chinese attitude arises out of the behaviour of the foreigner, not his racial origin.

[4] A third common reason for racial prejudice in the West, the foreigner's appropriation of 'our' women, may have been present. Indians in Burma or Chinese in Malaysia very seldom brought women with them, and married or cohabited with local girls. Those who were prosperous found little difficulty in attracting wives.

as freedom of the press and the liberty of the individual. The new higher western education was almost everywhere transmitted through a European language, predominantly English, so that English became a means of common communication for the newly emerging middle class of southern Asia. Thinking in English, the new professional class (lawyers, doctors, professors) demanded the rights and liberties of Englishmen. Many of the new university colleges and high schools were established by Christian missionaries, and the aspiring youth of Asia was exposed to Christian doctrines of social reform. The 'political' aspect of this teaching was accepted— such as emphasis upon the equality of man—but the missionaries' attack upon Asian religion and tradition was often fiercely resented. In India, *sati* (the burning alive of widows), child marriage and all caste discrimination were assailed; in China, polygamy and foot-binding. All too often, nineteenth-century Christianity appeared to postulate the superiority of the West over Asia, sometimes in a narrowly philistine spirit. Reaction followed: there was a reassertion of Asian values: the renaissance of Hinduism in the various Vedanta movements and a Buddhist revival in Ceylon and later in Burma.

Among the new levels of political and social leadership in South and East Asia a new doctrine took hold; a nationalism that seized upon the idea of 'national self-determination' and proclaimed the right of every people to be free from alien rule; a nationalism that revolted against western dominance and the exploitation of Asia by the West. This new nationalism was a compound of western political ideas, together with a rejection of western claims to superiority.

The growth of Asian middle-class nationalism was paralleled by an increasingly racial attitude among Europeans in Asia. The change should not be presented in absolute terms; there was no 'golden age' of East-West relations, followed by an age of iron; but there was an increasing sense that Europe (specifically Britain, of course, among the British) possessed a prescriptive right to rule the 'lesser breeds without the law'. This attitude has been ascribed in India to the British triumph in the Mutiny. But although the Mutiny accentuated the trend it was only one important factor among many.[5] At British

[5] For example Meredith Townsend, later editor of the *Spectator*, was writing in March 1857—before the Mutiny began—'All the parliaments in the world cannot make a native and a European equal.' Vide *Friend of India* newspaper, March 12, 1857.

universities, especially at Oxford, a new tone of authoritarianism was heard from political theorists like T. H. Green. A new emphasis laid upon government regulation, upon 'forcing men to be free', had its effect upon Oxford-trained Indian Civil Servants. Similarly, a crude interpretation of Darwin, concentrating upon the 'survival of the fittest', seemed to offer scientific warrant for a concept of racial supremacy based upon performance. And so a racial philosophy of character was formed; English were endowed with pluck, integrity, drive; Orientals were lacking in responsibility, indolent, corrupt, etc. This view of race as a moral determinant is well illustrated in Rudyard Kipling's work. Kipling was a racialist who yet believed in the regenerating power of the work of empire, whereby a Pathan outlaw might become a stalwart of the Guides Cavalry. In this way Gunga Din, the regimental water carrier, was able to attain the level of an Englishman. . . .

> *For all his dirty hide,*
> *He was white, clear white, inside . . .*

But the attainment of this moral 'whiteness' was not given to many Asians. In 1889, Lord Salisbury commented upon the attempt of Dadabhai Naoroji, the Parsee, to enter the House of Commons: 'I doubt if we have yet got to that point of view where a British constituency would elect a black man.' When reproached for his intolerance, Salisbury made things worse by explaining that, 'the colour is not exactly black, but at all events he is a man of another race'—this, it seems, implied a certain deficiency (nevertheless, Naoroji was duly elected). This elaboration of a racial attitude among Europeans towards Asians needs to be stated because many Asians were moved to retaliate by bitter attacks upon European rule and by asserting that Asia, unlike Europe, is free of racial feeling. Such a distinction is still maintained by many Asian intellectuals today.

British dominion in Asia originated in India, and it was extended by means of the Royal Navy and the Indian Army to Aden, East Africa, Burma, Malaya and Hongkong. The administration which followed drew upon Indian resources, and many of the large economic enterprises throughout this Indian Ocean area were British-Indian in origin. Thus, to supplement the small numbers of Gujarati and other merchants who had long represented the Indian community overseas, there now came a mass emigration of thousands of Indians—cooly labour, soldiers, technicians, clerks, moneylenders, and professional people—pouring into the British colonies of the Indian Ocean seaboard. Another and even greater flood of emigrants left southern China for the *Nan-Yang*, the 'South Seas'.[6] Most of these landed as poor coolies, but many made fortunes in these lands of opportunity. Many of the emigrants were absorbed into largely new economic sectors, Indians into tea and rubber estates, Chinese into tin-mines, and both into the oilfields. But some of the emigrants shouldered aside the indigenous peoples in agriculture and other pursuits. Often these emigrants were installed in positions of conspicuous power: in Malaya, the Tamil stationmaster, the Sikh policeman, the Chinese haulage operator, the Chettyar money-lender, the Chinese bank-official (the *comprador*); all were in a position to give or withhold favours from the country Malay, who resented these intruders into 'his' land. It is in this context of the 'plural society' that Asian racial tension chiefly is bred. Within the plural society the different races dwell, physically, alongside, yet hold no communication other than that of the market-place or the office counter where all too often one of the communities is conscious of being at a disadvantage. They are not conscious of common interests or loyalties or traditions: they are all too conscious of conflicting and competing interests and loyalties.

The struggle for national independence became sharply defined in the 1920s and '30s and attained its climax in the 1940s. The politically active middle class was united in a common cause, in the struggle with the colonial power for independence. To the suggestion advanced by some European writers that national unity was more a distant ideal than an immediate reality, they countered with charges against the imperial power of deliberately pursuing a policy of divide and rule, of setting differing religions and classes at each other's throats. In this atmosphere, any dispassionate assessment of

[6] Latest figures suggest that there are some 700,000 Indians in Malaya, and also 700,000 in Burma. In Ceylon there are 1,021,000 Indians; in Indonesia 27,000 and in Thailand, 20,000. Overseas Chinese include 2,300,000 in the Federation of Malaya and 920,000 in Singapore. Thailand has 3,000,000; Vietnam some 900,000; Indonesia, 2,200,000. There are 350,000 in Burma; 200,000 in the Philippines and 180,000 in Cambodia.

factors in national unity was impossible. Yet in some instances, as the withdrawal of the European overlord became ever more imminent, there was a drawing apart of political groups which had achieved a paper accord in days when independence had seemed more distant. This drawing apart especially affected the Muslims of India, who eventually formulated a demand for a separate nation-state. When the colonial power resisted the independence demand, as in Indonesia, a synthetic unity was preserved, but here also disunity has followed the departure of the European. Indeed, in most of the new countries of Southern Asia powerful forces are working against the new national unity, harking back to older loyalties.

One important cause is the attempt in almost all these former European dependencies to abolish the use of the language of the European in political institutions, the administration, the law and education. But if English and Dutch are discarded there is the problem of finding an acceptable substitute. Almost everywhere the proposed national language is the mother speech of a major population group, and it could in time develop into a genuine national tongue.[7] But the language fanatics cannot wait for natural processes to take effect. In India, Ceylon, Malaya and Burma, a national language has been imposed by political demand upon unwilling compatriots. There has been an attempt in Indonesia to create a new, synthetic speech, *bahasa Indonesia*, while in Pakistan the violent rivalry between Urdu and Bengali has led to a consideration of the use of Arabic as a possible compromise; but meanwhile English remains. The imposed language policy has led to determined resistance in India and Ceylon. The Tamils of Ceylon refuse to accept Sinhalese, particularly as they suspect (with some reason) that this is a device for paring down their leading share in government service and business. Throughout India there has been a surge of resentment against attempts to impose Hindi upon Bengalis, Marathas, Dravidians and others. Moreover, the Hindi champions have not been content to adopt 'Bazaar Hindi' which has some claim to be a lingua franca, but have sought to create an exclusive, literary Hindi

[7] The ascendancy of the East Midlands-London dialect in England was achieved only very gradually. The use of Norman French in courts of law was not finally discontinued until 1731. A last vestige persists today in the formula for acceding to legislation, 'Le Roy Le Veult'.

that omits all words of non-Sanskritic origin.[8] As a result of this linguistic authoritarianism, politics at the state level in India has become deeply riven by regional linguistic demands. In 1956, in response to regional pressure, the entire political map of India was reorganised on linguistic lines. In Madras new parties have emerged —and have won constituencies—based on a demand for an independent Tamil nation-state (the Dravida Munnetra Kazhagam is the most active of these parties).

The acceptance of Burmese as the national language of Burma offers far fewer problems: it is the mother speech of two-thirds of the population, and is readily understood by three-quarters. Yet even in Burma the Shans talk about secession, partly because of Burmese 'cultural imperialism'. The adoption of Malay as the national language of independent Malaya follows upon the use of Malay in the district administration and even in the councils of the sultans during the British period. Yet the Chinese in Malaya form a minority that may well be a majority within twenty years or less, and it remains to be seen how long they will tolerate the exclusion of their tongue from use in the administration and courts of law. The elections of May 1959 in Singapore (in which Chinese-language versus English-language education was an issue) appear to offer a warning that Chinese linguistic nationalism remains potent in Malaya.

The potency of language divisions in Asia as a source of quasi-racial conflicts was grimly illustrated by the Colombo riots of May 1958, when in three days of Tamil-Sinhalese conflict 300 were killed and 12,000 rendered homeless: this in a country that attained independence without any shedding of blood.

Equally potent as a source of communal conflict is religious bigotry. Islam appears to be specially susceptible to the cry of 'religion in danger', as the Lahore riots of 1953 demonstrated. The city of Lahore, together with other Punjab towns, was plunged into mob-anarchy over the issue of the Ahmadiyya, a Muslim dissident sect (heretic, some would say). Chief Justice Munir in his report after these riots observed: 'This inquiry has shown that the people

[8] Thus, the village accountant who has been called a *patwari* for 500 years has been renamed *lekhpal*. This is just as though in England purists were to demand that the term 'mayor' be abolished as a parvenu Norman intrusion in favour of 'moot-master' or some such contrived Anglo-Saxonism.

can be persuaded to go to any length in the name of religion.'
Islamic bigotry has shown itself in independent Malaya, though
receiving no countenance from the present government. In Indonesia, the *dar ul Islam* is only the most extreme of a number of
parties appealing to Muslims to establish the state upon Islamic
principles. In India, also, political agitation based upon religion is by
no means defunct, despite the poor showing of the communal Hindu
parties at elections. The Buddhist lands of South-East Asia generally
reflect the tolerance and charitableness of their faith; but occasionally
sections of the monks will endeavour to bring religion into politics,
as in the monastic agitation of September 1954 against Islamic
teaching in state-supported schools in Burma. In South-East Asia,
pseudo-racial divisions along religious lines have most often arisen
in relation to militant Christian minorities. The Karens in Burma
have folk memories of ancient hostility with the Burmese, but their
continuing sense of separateness was undoubtedly accentuated by
the Christian cultural separation of their leaders and their identification with British authority, through the mediation of the missionaries. Similarly, the Ambonese and other Christian communities in
Indonesia (such as the Minado of Celebes) have found most difficulty
in coming to terms with the new republic. The position of the
Roman Catholic community of Vietnam is not dissimilar.

Finally, problems of racialism (or, more properly, tribalism)
arise with regard to groups which were until recently upon the
fringes of colonial rule, largely insulated from its transforming
influences. The Naga tribes of the Assam-Burma border, brought
under only the loosest kind of British administration, now resent
Indian attempts to extend the scope of authority; the Nagas demand
their own separate Naga state. The Pathan tribes which straddle the
Durand Line between Pakistan and Afghanistan are still Afridi,
Mahsud or Mohmand first; Muslims second; and nationals of a
twentieth-century polity only so far as suits them. The Muslim
tribes of Sulu and Mindanao, similarly, belong to a frontier area
that takes little account of the political boundary between the Philippines and Borneo. Some might argue that the Tibetans are only the
largest of these isolated pockets of folk whom time has passed by;
frontier societies which are now being rudely forced to conform to
the international boundaries of the twentieth century.

If within the new countries of southern Asia there are many

fissiparous forces there are also important ties that bind together. Most of the new nations have chosen to undertake programmes of economic expansion by means of state support, state enterprise (nationalised industry) and state planning. State planning and investment have a dual effect. State control and direction almost inevitably entail centralisation: they also encourage a nationwide view, the planners are compelled to consider national income and national production and to see the whole country as one integrated economy. Yet planning in its Olympian remoteness, its wide-ranging consequences, can awaken sectional dissatisfaction. Every state in India finds it necessary to demonstrate its discontent with the allocations of the Planning Commission by exceeding the development budget laid down by the centre. For many years, East Pakistan contrasted the generous allotments for industrial develop-ment to the western wing with the meagre doles to the east. The neglect of Arakan by the central government in Rangoon was a prime cause of the formation of a separatist Arakanese party. The alleged concentration of development in Java (at the expense of oil revenues earned by Sumatra) was a considerable grievance leading to the 1957 rising in Sumatra and the setting up of a separate revolu-tionary government. Yet even though it is necessary to enumerate this list of planning failures, in the long run planning and develop-ment should serve to draw together the separate regions within the nation. There are other, less equivocal forces. National political parties can unite leaders of varying regional cultures within one common organisation and programme. The Muslim League, before it fell into decay, offered the surprising phenomenon of Oudh land-lords, Bengali schoolmasters and Punjabi yeomen-farmers united behind the leadership of an Anglicised Bombay barrister in the common cause of Muslim rights. The Congress in India, despite regional stresses, continues to draw together men of differing faiths, differing tongues and differing social and economic status. In Malaya, for however long, upper middle-class Malay and Chinese politicians have been able to form an 'Alliance' party that has successfully steered the country into independence, despite the absence of any tangible cultural or even economic bond between them. Perhaps even more vital as a factor for unity are the national civil service and the fighting services. The young administrator or army officer is selected on a basis of fitness; he is conscious (perhaps too conscious) that he belongs to an élite, in which social or regional origin is of little account. He will learn the national language and employ it in his work.[9] He will almost certainly be posted to districts far from his home, and he will be engaged upon duties which have a national and not a local significance. The major universities also provide a unifying influence. At the University of the Philippines, or the University of Malaya, students and staff rub shoulders with colleagues from every part of their own country and from overseas and become conscious of a wider empathy. The press and the radio are also forces acting for unity whose influence has only just begun. Similarly, better communications are breaking down the particularism of yesterday. Only thirty years ago, many South Asian peasants never visited more than a dozen miles from their village (except, maybe, for an occasional religious pilgrimage). Now, the ubiquitous country bus offers the opportunity of cheap travel to all. On another level, air travel has helped to bridge the vast distances of Asia as the train never could.

In tracing the broadening of loyalties from ancient village or tribal particularism towards the attainment of national unity, it is necessary to turn aside and notice the emergence of a different pattern in China. In the past there was the Confucian model of civilised relations, to which the non-Han minorities and the frontier peoples were forcibly compelled to conform. The only mitigation of the Sinoisation policy lay in the frequent inability of the central government to enforce its mandate over the fringe territories of the Middle Kingdom, as in Tibet for many centuries. The Kuomintang régime renewed this traditional policy and Chiang Kai-shek's political testament, *China's Destiny*, was notably xenophobic. The communist government reversed the whole policy of cultural Sinoisation: the non-Han peoples were encouraged through festivals and other means to give expression to their own arts and crafts, while the study of regional languages has been fostered in schools and universities. Varying degrees of political devolution were bestowed upon the minorities: the largest units are the five Autonomous Regions extended to the Mongol, Uighur and other races. This appears to follow the established Soviet policy of creating republics in Central Asia representing linguistic or racial entities, such as Kazakhstan.

[9] The Pakistani civil service probationer has to learn the language of the wing to which he does not belong: e.g., Urdu, if he is a Bengali.

This policy is designed to by-pass the basic dilemma of western colonial rule: the rise of nationalism, feeding upon the political tradition of the colonial power, but anti-colonial. The Soviets have avoided the issue of racial distinction at least on the surface by not setting apart the Russians as a ruling race. It may be that a majority of the higher government officials and technicians in Central Asia are European Russians but they were—they say—selected purely for their party or professional qualifications. And in addition there are millions of other Russians in Central Asia (specially young people) who are working with their hands in agriculture or industry at a social and economic level no different to that of a Kazhak or Turki labourer. Whatever resentments may lie beneath the surface, outwardly there is an appearance of equality. Will the People's Republic of China be successful in creating a communist order in which nationalism is merged in unity? Tibet appears to represent a denial, but these are early days; there were revolts in Central Asian republics soon after the Soviet revolution.

Meanwhile, nationalism is the political fashion in South and East Asia. The leaders of the newly independent countries are intensely determined to establish their parity with older states, rather like German and Italian statesmen and publicists in the nineteenth century. So far, nationalism is most articulate in continuing the battle with the departed European imperial powers. Indonesian unity can be given a fillip by raising the issue of Irian Bharat or West New Guinea under Dutch rule, and later by 'confrontation' against a Malaysia allegedly British-dominated. Suez, as an apparent effort to reassert British and French dominance in the Middle East, provoked a united and spontaneous protest from southern Asia—a protest by people in crowds, rather than by governments. The growth of a Pan-Asian movement—the Bandung African-Asian Conference, and its successors—has hinged upon anti-colonial unanimity, and almost on that alone. Apart from opposition to colonialism, international opinion in Asia coalesces on the problem of economic development. The UN is valued for its economic and technical agencies, but perhaps more as an organisation in which the powerless have an authority equal to that of the powerful. Fear of stronger neighbours (Ceylon's fear of India, Thailand's of China, Cambodia's of Thailand, etc.) is certainly a factor in foreign relations, but this fear is seldom categorically stated, whereas misgivings about the

West are almost always overstated. Within the Asian family only one country, Japan, looks out at the world with cool realism.[10] Those who will trade will be cultivated, whatever continent or island they belong to. But almost every other non-communist Asian country is still wrapped in a mantle of suspicion of the old imperialists (Britain, France, Portugal, the Netherlands) and the new juggernaut, the United States. This image of western Europe and America as protagonists in a system that means inequality and oppression is, however, not applied by Asians to individuals of these countries. There is hostility to foreign policy; sometimes hostility to the material evidence of this policy (as to the personnel of American military bases) and occasionally to manifestations of economic imperialism, such as oil companies. But the individual Englishman or American is treated with courtesy, unless he is quite unusually offensive in his behaviour. Racial prejudice against westerners is occasionally artificially stimulated by propaganda (as in the time of the expulsion of the Dutch from Indonesia), but despite the fierce struggle of Asian nationalism against western colonialism during the last two decades, a white skin is not today a disability in Asia. Indeed, the Englishman returning to independent India meets with nothing but friendship. Colour, as such, is not an appreciable cause of racial intolerance in Asia. The threat of discrimination or violence lies most in religious or economic pressures. Religion has always provided a latent source of communal discord in Asia, and religion allied to a crude nationalism is even more inflammable. The conflict which accompanied the transfer of power in India, when some fifteen million Hindus, Muslims and Sikhs were driven from their homes, while perhaps half a million were killed, was only the most terrible of recent clashes. The economic factor is often exposed in reaction against the commercial domination of the foreigner, which is even more resented in this day when economic exploitation is often regarded as the greatest evil of colonialism. Thus the Chettyar community of money-lenders who come from south India have seen their land-holdings in Burma expropriated and their credit operations virtually brought to an end. In several other South-East Asian countries, in Thailand, the Philippines and South Vietnam,

[10] But the conclusion of a defence agreement between Japan and the United States in 1960 was the signal for one of the most violent outbursts against American dominance yet seen in Asia.

draconian measures have been taken against the resident Chinese communities with their large-scale control over commerce and industry.

The conclusion which this writer draws from a survey of 'race' relations in Asia is that, despite special circumstances and the special forms assumed by nationalism and communalism, the problem in Asia reflects the universal problem. Almost every one of the situations analysed above could be duplicated in European history, and many in the Americas. If Asia has been spared the tragedy of Africa it is because historical development, particularly economic development, has evolved differently. To isolate one element, nowhere has a powerful planter or *baas* community emerged as a separate racial group with the ambition of seizing the strings of government. But this does not mean that Asians are cast in a different mould in their response to racial or nationalistic impulses: human nature is not different in Asia. The integration of the Harijan, the former untouchable, in India is just as much a 'racial' problem as the integration of the Negro in the United States.

9

Magnificent Failure?

THE GANDHIAN IDEAL IN INDIA

'POSTERITY will probably rate Gandhi as one of history's magnificent failures': so says Frank Moraes, editor-in-chief of the *Express* group of Indian newspapers, in his book *India To-day*. He goes on to qualify this asseveration somewhat, but he concludes that 'the new class he created over thirty years of undisputed leadership' (that is, the Congress 'Freedom Fighters', drawn from the literary, professional middle class, pledged to work for independence) 'jettisoned his economic and political ideas within a decade of his death'. Service, Moraes declares, has given way to a struggle for power and privilege: 'By and large the new class has turned its back on most of Gandhi's cherished ideals; and ironically it has done so under the inspiration of the Mahatma's chosen heir.'[1] Writing on the anniversary of Gandhi's birthday, *The Times* correspondent in Delhi concluded, in October 1963: 'It has been said that Gandhi waged two struggles, against the British Raj and against his own people, and his second adversary was the more obdurate.'[2] 'Lead Kindly Light' was Gandhi's favourite hymn; was his a light that failed?

Probably nobody would have been more ready than Gandhi himself to have accepted the indictment on the failure of his life's

[1] Frank Moraes, *India To-day*, New York, 1960, pp. 89–91.
[2] *The Times*, October 3, 1963.

mission. He was always almost morbidly conscious of falling below his own standards. He threw up his first case because he was dissatisfied with his efforts. Time and again he confessed that his followers fell short of the ideal of non-violence: as after the Amritsar tragedy (1919), after the Chauri Chaura killings (1922), and right at the end of his life when he declared: 'My eyes have now been opened. I see that what we practised during the fight with the British under the name of non-violence, was not really non-violence' (December 1947).

Gandhi's political philosophy was essentially individual, radiated through mind and action and not at all through an ideological programme, still less through a political party or political institutions. Hence, it is peculiarly vulnerable to the passing of time. Gandhi attempted to work through his immediate disciples, and through the Indian masses as his ultimate followers, with virtually no fixed organisation and with something like indifference to the normal end of politics, that is, power. During Gandhi's lifetime, millions called him *Bapu*, Father. When he was removed from the scene, the movement was dependent upon the continuing faithfulness of those he had looked upon as sons. But even before his death, his disciples had, almost all, been lured by the challenge of power. They did not turn their backs on Gandhi. Not at all; instead, they elevated him into a deity. Gandhi used to reply to eager Christians, who urged him to become one of them, that whereas the Sermon on the Mount was the foundation of his thinking, it formed no part of Christian practice. In the same way the Gandhian ethic, the theory or ideal of that modern India which Arthur Koestler terms a 'Bapucracy', is neither practised nor even understood by many of the politicians who evoke his name like a *mantra* or talisman.

Yet contemporary India bears, unmistakably, the Gandhian stigmata. At every level of politics and society, gladly or sadly, people witness to the influence of Gandhi. Only one country known to the present writer has succeeded in carrying through the dream of the 'Freedom Struggle' into the reality of independence: Israel. If in India the dream has faded, the Gandhian spirit of dedication survives, however distorted or submerged. While many among the governing class invoke the name of Gandhi with meaningless unction, others are perceptibly troubled by his memory. The little people still warm themselves in the glow of his countenance, as once they cherished the protecting if distant affection of Queen Victoria. And a few seekers after truth attempt to re-create the Gandhian vision of society which somehow eluded the Mahatma in his latter years.

The Gandhian student who attempts to find the man and the message at the centre of the myth does not lack working material. Just as there are as many Hamlets as there are actors, so from a hundred pens there have appeared a hundred interpretations. Even if the attempt is made to approach the man through his own writing, this is so voluminous that the tyro is constrained to avail himself of the labours of those who have previously worked through the Gandhian corpus in detail. Sooner rather than later the Gandhian student will turn to the 'official' biography by D. G. Tendulkar, *Mahatma*, recently reissued in a second and revised edition.[3] The author began his great work during the lifetime of his subject, and was able to consult him on many points. The first edition appeared during the years 1951–4, during the brave years of the First Five Year Plan, when internal development was going well ahead while India's stature as a moral force on the international scene was at its height. The second edition was issued during the dismal 1960s, when democracy, development and non-alignment have all been tried and found wanting in India. Yet, although the author tells us that this was a 'completely revised edition', it was in fact essentially the same. This no doubt was inevitable. When one has laboured to produce eight volumes in sequence, one is so committed to a particular form of presentation that no major reassessment can be contemplated.

Tendulkar's attitude is poised between adoration of the *deva* and nostalgia for the 'Freedom Struggle'. On the title-page of all the eight volumes is inscribed an invocation to the *deva*:

He is the One Luminous, Creator of All, Mahatma, ...
Whoever knows Him, Immortal becomes.

The first chapter of the first volume is headed "Plassey to Amritsar". This is shorthand for 'From the beginning to the ending of British

[3] *Mahatma: Life of Mohandas Karamchand Gandhi*, Vols. I–VIII, rev. ed. by D. G. Tendulkar, foreword by Jawaharlal Nehru, Delhi, 1960–3.

overlordship: The Saga of the Freedom Struggle'. Both these events
were anathema to Gandhi. Plassey revealed the moral bankruptcy of
the old India; Amritsar revealed the false values of the new India,
based in fear and hatred. Yet, to the Indian nationalist—in 1951 or
in 1965—the 'Freedom Struggle' remains the great epic, the great
adventure. Independence may have turned sour, but the exhilarating
memory of the great days remains: the great days when to be arres-
ted by a British inspector was to attain the heights of self-sacrifice—
and nympholepsy. . . .

> *Now that's all shoved behind me —*
> *Long ago and far away.*

Tendulkar's task is to ensure that the long ago is always with us;
that the 'Freedom Struggle', though long since over, is fought again
and again.

The interpretations of Gandhi which confront the student
almost all fall into the twin categories of those who saw him as a
religious phenomenon, and those who regarded him as the symbol
of the fight against imperialism. In the first category, beside his
Indian devotees, there were his English friends, C. F. Andrews,
Edward Thompson and Horace Alexander: Christians of a unique
persuasion. Most of his Asian and American biographers come into
the second category, as anti-colonialists. No doubt we in the '60s
were as much shackled to the viewpoint of our own time as the men
of 1924 or 1944. But now it is just a little easier to begin to see
Gandhi in a wider perspective. This is surely the first lesson to be
learned: that although contemporary India has the glory of being
Gandhi's land, by ancestry and by choice, he belongs to himself and
to all the world.

When India was plunged into the elections of 1936—the vital
elections which were to be the parting of the ways between the
Congress and the Muslim League—Gandhi retired to a one-room
mud hut in the village of Segaon, eleven miles from Wardha. One
day he was visited by a Polish engineer, Maurice Frydman, who
asked him if his purpose in settling in Segaon was humanitarian.
Gandhi replied: 'I am here to serve no one but myself; to find my
own self-realisation through the service of these village folk. Man's
ultimate aim is the realisation of God, and all his activities, political,
social and religious, have to be guided by the ultimate aim of the

vision of God. . . . I am a part and parcel of the whole, and I cannot find him apart from the rest of humanity. My countrymen are my nearest neighbours. They have become so helpless, resourceless and inert that I must concentrate on serving them. If I could persuade myself that I should find him in a Himalayan cave, I would proceed there immediately. But I know that I cannot find him apart from humanity.'[4]

Was there ever such an individual quest for God and truth as that followed by Gandhi? Hindus, Christians, Buddhists, Marxists —all claim the Mahatma for themselves. But he found what he wanted where he wanted. He relates that the first great influence was the Sermon on the Mount. This he discovered for himself before he found the message of the *Gita*. The *Bhagavad Gita*, the greatest influence in his life, he first read in Sir Edwin Arnold's paraphrase, *The Song Celestial*. The significance of Islam, of submission to God, first came to him via Carlyle's essay, *Hero as Prophet*, which led him to read the *Koran* in English translation. When Polak gave Gandhi *Unto This Last* by John Ruskin, he read the book through and could not sleep for exaltation. At the end of his days he averred 'That book marked the turning-point in my life.'[5] He translated *Unto This Last* himself, under the prophetic title, *Sarvodaya*, or *Universal Dawn*.

When we read Ruskin, what do we find? There is a castigation of classical *laisser faire* political economy; an insistence upon the 'moral sign' attached to wealth—an insistence that people are wealth—that rich and poor meet under God, that co-operation means life and competition means death; that to be 'valuable' is to avail towards life, and that true wealth is the possession of the valuable by the valiant. Industrialisation is dismissed as a blind alley: 'Men can neither drink steam nor eat stone.' England may become one vast manufacturing town, 'but the world cannot become a factory, nor a mine'. The final test is this: 'How much clear use for food, knowledge, or joy, this that you have bought can be put.' All this can readily be seen as fundamental to Gandhian philosophy: yet how much richer *sarvodaya* becomes than Ruskin's plea for a morality beyond the economic price! Ruskin provides Gandhi not with an intellectual platform, but with an intellectual spring-board.

[4] Tendulkar, Vol. IV, p. 88.
[5] Tendulkar, Vol. VIII, p. 239.

Out of Ruskin's conclusion 'Government and co-operation are in all things the laws of life', Gandhi creates his concept of *sarvodaya*, the 'Welfare of All'; the politics of co-operation, of humanity. He had made his first great discovery in his 'Experiments with Truth' ten years before he had opened *Unto This Last*. His first visit to South Africa was on behalf of Dada Abdulla & Co., a family of Muslim Memon merchants. After a year's preliminaries, Gandhi concluded that his client had a strong case, but he perceived that litigation might ruin plaintiff and defendant—both being relatives from the same town, Porbander. He therefore deemed it his duty to bring both parties together, and to find a means whereby the debtor, Tyeb Sheth, could discharge his debt without failing in his business. Gandhi concludes: 'Both were happy in the result and both rose in the public estimation. My joy was boundless. I had learnt the true practice of law. . . . I realised that the true function of a lawyer was to unite parties riven asunder. The lesson was so indelibly burnt into me that a large part of my time during the twenty years of my practice as a lawyer was occupied in bringing about private compromises of hundreds of cases.'[6]

Compromise: conciliation: co-operation: this was the essence of Gandhi's political creed. In the submission of this writer this is the key to Gandhi's hold upon the masses of India. The extent to which independent India has furthered this creed is the true measurement of Gandhi's success or failure.

The compromise incident is passed over by Tendulkar in three lines, without comment. Struggle, not compromise, is his theme.[7] Indeed, Tendulkar spares only one volume for the first fifty years of Gandhi's life. Volume 2 carries the narrative forward another nine years, and thereafter the time-scale narrows until the last volume covers only eight months. This allocation is clearly influenced by the problem of coping with the multifarious materials of the last few years. Comprehension, not selection, has been the guiding principle.

[6] Gandhi, *An Autobiography: The Story of My Experiments with Truth*, London, 1949, p. 112.

[7] B. R. Nanda also appears to miss the significance of this incident. See his *Mahatma Gandhi: An Autobiography*, London, 1958, p. 41. It has been left to Susanne Rudolph to place this episode centrally in Gandhi's development; see "Conflict and Consensus in Indian Politics", *World Politics*, April 1961.

However, this is also a value judgement; these were the years (1930–1947) when the Congress was India and Gandhi was the Congress: the years of harvest. But much more significant were the early years of sowing. It can plausibly be argued that when Gandhi left South Africa in 1914 his whole political philosophy had been developed, tested and articulated. Thereafter, he suffered failures and disappointments. But all the positive thinking had been completed. It is all there: the co-operative society where intellectuals and manual workers find a common purpose, first at Phoenix and then at Tolstoy Farm; the attempt to give self-respect to those whom tradition has handicapped, women and the low of caste; the philosophy and technique of non-violence, and the readiness to meet and compromise with the adversary who appeals to trust. There was even the incident of the man of violence who could not understand Ghandian compromise, and so turned upon his former leader, striking him down, so that he fell with the words *He Rama* on his lips: Gandhi's 'Eloi, Eloi, lama sabachthani?'

At the end of it all, Gandhi had discovered: 'You cannot serve God and Mammon is an economic truth of the highest value. We have to make our choice. Western nations are groaning under the monster-god of materialism. Their moral growth has become stunted. . . . Under the British *aegis* we have learnt much, but it is my firm belief that, if we are not careful, we shall introduce all the vices that she has been a prey to owing to the disease of materialism. . . . Let us first seek the Kingdom of God and his righteousness, and the irrevocable promise is that everything will be added unto us. These are real economics.'[8] And, Gandhi could have added, real politics. His view was somewhat longer than that of Osagyefo Dr Nkrumah, the seeker after the political kingdom.

Gandhi left South Africa with the ideal intact. Thousands of indentured Indians had followed him in *satyagraha*, and had obeyed his instructions implicitly. Never again was the Kingdom of God to be fully realised through popular action. From this time forward Gandhi was compelled to face the problem of accepting less than the ideal. He did not easily climb down. After Amritsar, Rabindranath Tagore wrote to Gandhi: 'The great gift of freedom can never come to a people through charity . . . India's opportunity for

[8] Tendulkar, Vol. I, p. 197.

winning it will come to her when she can prove that she is morally superior to the people who rule by their strength of conquest.' In this spirit, Gandhi repudiated the violence in the Punjab and declared: 'We must fearlessly spread the doctrine of *satya* [sacrifice] and *ahimsa* [harmlessness] and then, not till then we shall be able to undertake mass *satyagraha*.'[9]

Within two years he had launched another *satyagraha* campaign. Again, this degenerated into violence, and Gandhi terminated the movement, confessing to a Himalayan blunder. He was learning much that was bitter. His great mass movement of 1920–1 was launched in support of the Muslim Khalifat agitation. What better demonstration could there be of the politics of co-operation than a campaign for a purpose which had no direct interest to the Hindus, the majority of Congress supporters, in protest not against material grievances but against betrayal by the Lloyd George government of solemn British pledges? After the first raptures of intercommunal co-operation, breaches began to appear between different groups within the Congress and within the Hindu-Muslim alliance. Still we find him in 1924 working for co-operation. He writes in *Young India*: 'I have therefore suggested that we should find out the lowest common measure among all the political parties and invite them all to co-operate on the Congress platform for achieving their common measure.'[10]

While to Gandhi and Nehru and other visionaries the Congress was the symbol of Indian unity, to their lesser followers it was the means whereby they could first seize power from the British and then exploit power for purposes which they—as Hindus, as socialists, or whatever—deemed right. The vision of a common purpose was beyond them. A prime example may be seen in the language movement. Congress believed that India must rediscover her true nature through discarding the English language as the medium of public life, higher education and cultural exchange, and return to *swabhasha*, the mother tongue. For a common, all-India language, Hindustani, the lingua franca of northern India, with its Sanskritic base, its vocabulary drawing upon Urdu and other cosmopolitan sources, and its Hindu and Muslim literary affiliations, was the natural choice. Hindu zealots took over this proposition and worked to substitute, for the unifying Hindustani, a divisive Hindi written

[9] Tendulkar, Vol. I, pp. 260, 262.   [10] Tendulkar, Vol. II, p. 146.

in the Devanagari script, and purged of all non-Sanskritic words. Gandhi never accepted this divagation: in August 1947 he still insisted upon 'Hindustani, the lingua franca of India written in the Nagari or the Urdu script. This is neither Sanskritised Hindi nor Persianised Urdu. Hindustani is emphatically the language which is spoken by the millions north of the Vindhya range.'[11]

While the philologist might jib at the last proposition, the nationalist could only applaud its sentiment. Yet ten years before Gandhi made this last declaration for a unifying national language, Congress leaders began to enforce a policy of imposing Sanskritised Hindi in public life and public education, thereby precipitating the trend towards linguistic regionalism and linguistic separatism which has since eroded the subcontinent. At the same time, in order to retain his influence within a Congress that was increasingly responding to the pressure of the Hindu zealots, Gandhi was constrained to speak in accents of appeal: so we find him inclining towards the Nagari script (which, of course, he himself used), describing Persian terms in Hindustani as 'artificial and unnatural', and insisting that between his version of Hindustani and Hindi there was little difference. To those Muslims now ready to see evil in every act or statement of a Congress leader, these were the items which mattered; not the continuing advocacy of Hindustani.

Gandhi continued to the end to work for reconciliation. On 4 October 1946, he issued a joint statement with the Nawab of Bhopal declaring: 'It is understood that all the ministers of the Interim government will work as a team for the good of the whole of India and will never invoke the intervention of the governor-general in any case.'[12] Amid the darkening gloom of enmity between Congress and the Muslim League, Gandhi's plea for a morality higher than party politics left both sides unmoved. The Interim government was a house divided: it could not long stand. Lord Wavell as viceroy continued to work to bring the Congress and the League together, but in February 1947 he was replaced by Lord Mountbatten, who brought to his task the sense that:

> If it were done, when 'tis done, then 'twere well
> It were done quickly.

[11] Tendulkar, Vol. VIII, p. 84.
[12] Tendulkar, Vol. VII, p. 230.

What followed is told by V. P. Menon in his *Transfer of Power in India*:

> In his very first interview with Lord Mountbatten, Gandhiji suggested that the viceroy should dismiss the existing cabinet and give Jinnah the option of forming a new one; that the selection of the members should be left to Jinnah—they might be all Muslims or all non-Muslims, or they might be representatives of all classes and creeds. If Jinnah accepted the offer, the Congress would guarantee to co-operate freely and sincerely, so long as all the measures that the cabinet might bring forward were in the interests of the Indian people as a whole. The sole referee of what was, or was not, in the interests of India as a whole would be Lord Mountbatten in his personal capacity. Jinnah should undertake on behalf of the League, or of any other parties represented in the cabinet, that they would do their utmost to preserve peace throughout India. . . . Jinnah would be perfectly at liberty to plan for Pakistan and even to put his plans into effect before the transfer of power, provided that he was successful in appealing to reason and did not use force.[13]

This offer was almost immediately repudiated by the Congress, and Gandhi withdrew from the negotiations, leaving the field to the Working Committee, the high command of the Congress. Had it been accepted by the Congress and by Jinnah it might have prevented what, in retrospect, looks like the irrevocable parting between Hindus and Muslims in India. It is difficult to find parallel examples of magnanimity in history. We think of General Grant at Appomattox, bidding the Confederate soldiers go back to their farms with their horses; or of Botha and Smuts responding to Campbell-Bannerman's hand held out in friendship. But these reconciliations took place when the issue was decided, the conflict over. Gandhi made his effort towards reconciliation when the conflict was at its climax. The fledgling lawyer who advised compromise to a client who had a winning case, and the elderly politician who tried to put a triumphant party into the hands of a weaker opponent are one and the same—except that the young lawyer prevailed upon his client

[13] V. P. Menon, *The Transfer of Power in India*, London and Princeton, 1957, pp. 352–3.

and the elderly politician failed to persuade his party: a magnificent failure.

This attempted reconciliation, which may properly be regarded as the culmination of Gandhi's effort to put morality into politics, is not mentioned by Tendulkar. It was just possible that at the time of writing his original work he was not aware of the incident (though he claims to have been at Gandhi's elbow at this time), but no such excuse can be offered for its omission from the second edition. It seems clear that those who see events in terms of the 'Freedom Struggle' just do not wish to understand the Gandhian message. Even B. R. Nanda, with his wider view, dismisses this event with the observation that 'the time for gestures was past'.[14] Does he really mean that, by 1947, the time for Gandhi was past, at the level of Congress leadership?

It is clear that Gandhi realised what a decline from absolute standards the pursuit of power had wrought in his colleagues and followers. In December 1947, in conversation with Dr Zakir Hussain, later vice-president of the Republic of India, Gandhi admitted: 'Today, everybody in the Congress is running after power.... The Congressmen failed to come up to scratch and to shoulder the burden. Such is our bankruptcy.... The objective of the constructive work organisation is to generate political power. But if we may say that political power, having come, it must be ours as a prize for our labours, it would degrade us and spell our ruin.'[15] On the eve of his last fast, in the month before his death, Gandhi read passages from an old friend's letter: 'The one great problem ... is the moral degradation into which the men in Congress circles have fallen.... The taste for political power has turned their heads.... Swaraj was the only self-absorbing passion.... But now that goal has been reached, all moral restrictions have lost their power on most of the fighters in the great struggle.'[16] Recognising that the Congress had succumbed to the corruption of power, like every other successful political movement, Gandhi turned away from the party with which he was so completely identified, and through which he had worked, and returned to the ideal from which they had lapsed. 'Purify yourselves of all dross. Banish the very idea

[14] *Op. cit.*, p. 503.
[15] Tendulkar, Vol. VIII, pp. 229, 230.
[16] Tendulkar, Vol. VIII, p. 248.

of capture of power and keep it on the right path. Therein lies salvation. There is no other way.'[17]

Although his kingdom was not of this world, Gandhi still worked for this world. Having failed to bring together the Congress and the League he succeeded in reconciling the ordinary people, Muslims and Hindus, in Calcutta and elsewhere in the face of blind religious hatred. Although Pakistan represented the antithesis of his hopes for all-India co-operation he led the way in calling for recognition and friendship for Pakistan. Almost his last message, dictated on 14 January 1948, was a plea for reconciliation, and for humanity beyond power.

'What should we do then? If we would see our dream of *panchayat raj*, that is true democracy, realised, we would regard the humblest and the lowest Indian as being equally the ruler of India with the tallest in the land. This presupposes that all are pure, or will become pure, if they are not. And purity must go hand in hand with wisdom.... Everybody would regard all as equal with oneself and would hold them together in the silken net of love.... Everybody would know how to earn an honest living by the sweat of one's brow and make no distinction between the intellectual and physical labour.'[18]

'I will give unto this last even as unto thee....' Few political leaders have been so fundamentally consistent as Gandhi, with a consistency impossible of achievement, even for the Mahatma himself. It is no surprise that he eludes his biographers and commentators, when in spirit he eluded himself. It is not surprising that the Gandhian ideal has not survived unblemished after sixteen years of independence: what is more surprising is that this ideal has not been eclipsed completely. Yet, as we shall discover, the 'dream of *panchayat raj*' is not altogether a mirage. 'That state will be the best which is governed the least', declared Gandhi, and 'Society based on non-violence can only consist of groups settled in villages in which voluntary co-operation is the condition of dignified and peaceful existence.... The nearest approach to civilisation based on non-violence is the erstwhile village republic of India.'[19] During the

[17] Tendulkar, Vol. VIII, p. 234.

[18] Tendulkar, Vol. VIII, pp. 253–4.

[19] S. N. Agarwal, *Gandhian Constitution for Free India*, Allahabad, 1946, pp. 39, 58.

first decade of independence, the power of the central government, far from declining, was deliberately reinforced. Yet there were many voices raised against the betrayal of Gandhian ideals in the Constituent Assembly and after.[20] What was first a protest became increasingly an affirmation of the positive superiority of *sarvodaya* over western representative democracy.

Much that Gandhi foresaw has come to pass: the faction and power-seeking in politics, especially. Would he have minded more that, as Frank Moraes suggests, his own trusted lieutenant, Jawaharlal Nehru, deliberately took the path of centralisation and industrialisation? The greatest departure from the Gandhian ideal has certainly been the pursuit of the material standards of the West by means of the western techniques of industrialisation: the attempt to turn India into a factory and a mine. Gandhi was quite certain that India should go no further than to accept the sewing-machine and the factory for making these machines. Even this was a falling short of the ideal. Confronted by an India which had already proceeded far towards industrialisation, Gandhi was prepared to concede that existing textile mills must be allowed to continue. When the provincial Congress governments first took office in 1946, Shri Prakasam, chief minister of Madras, announced that no new mills would be erected in his province. This Gandhi welcomed. For the existing mills under private ownership he advocated trusteeship: 'He wanted a peaceful conversion of millowners, so that the millowners and their employees would come under the social control voluntarily. . . . In one of the Tata concerns, the labourers were reported to have become profit-sharers. He considered such a solution to be the best.'[21]

One of the more sinister aspects of India in the sixties was the octopus-like extension of big-business control over industry, commerce and the communications network of newspapers. Whatever moral restraint Gandhi might have exercised over the Marwari and Parsee millionaires has not prevailed. In a society committed to planning, they retain the extra-social, irresponsible power of the American oil barons in their heyday. Although industrial develop-

[20] See the present writer's "Tradition and Experiment in Forms of Government" in C. H. Philips (ed.), *Politics and Society in India*, London and New York, 1963.

[21] Tendulkar, Vol. VII, p. 224.

ment has proceeded under formal public control, Indian industrial expansion has exhibited most of the ugly features of nineteenth-century western industrialisation. Millions of countryfolk have been sucked into the swollen industrial cities where their sole function is to provide units of production. The industrial shanty-towns and *bastis* have erupted and suppurated within and around the older cities with virtually no intervention, or sense of aroused responsibility emanating from industrialists or politicians. Between 1951 and 1961, the population of towns with 20,000 inhabitants or more rose by 40 per cent. The shortage of houses in cities and towns, estimated at 2,500,000 in 1951, was believed to have risen to 5,000,000 by 1961 (there are no reliable statistics). In the face of this swelling tide of rootless and roofless humanity, the sole palliative attempted has been the setting up of a metropolitan planning organisation in Calcutta under the auspices of WHO, the World Bank and the Ford Foundation.[22] Surely the constant expansion of industry combined with an almost total disregard for the human consequences would have most excited Gandhi's indignation in India today?

Equally anathema to Gandhi would have been the extreme centralisation promoted by the National Planning Commission. Although virtually outside the constitution, the Planning Commission represents the most powerful excrescence on the body politic to be found anywhere in the 'free world': though the Central Intelligence Agency in Washington in its prime must be considered a close contender. The Commission has given birth to a number of ancillary organisations whose activities extend into the whole range of the national life. The consequences of what one opposition party, *Swatantra*, calls 'non-responsible super-government' in elaborate and costive controls and in the setting up of national targets for development (which are seldom attained) upon the psychology of India, are far-reaching. Would Gandhi have tolerated the substitution of a system of control far greater than any under British rule in the name of *swaraj*?

The sphere in which Gandhian influence is often said to be paramount is foreign policy.[23] Of course, the philosophy of non-

[22] See *The Times*, December 5, 1963.
[23] See, for example, W. Range, *Jawaharlal Nehru's World View*, Athens, Georgia, 1961. 'His goal seems to be to adapt Gandhi's teachings to international relations' (p. viii).

alignment, of 'positive neutralism', derives directly from Gandhian teaching. How much more positive would Gandhi's own policy have been in action? Above all, Gandhi would have welcomed the *rapprochement* between India and Britain. Yet would he not have stimulated India into playing a more positive role in transforming the old unequal relationship into a partnership of trust? Would he not have sensed the potentialities of the Commonwealth as a world bridge, and have worked to extend the Commonwealth even wider, reclaiming countries such as Burma and Israel into partnership, and even perhaps bringing into the association other lands which have interests in common, as the Colombo Plan has done on a limited basis?

Yet the departures from Gandhi which have marked India's external relations cannot be ignored. Neutralism has been most convincing in inverse ratio to the direct involvement of Indian interests. Whether Gandhi would have countenanced a military invasion of Hyderabad may be doubted; he would certainly have condemned the invasion of Goa at least as forcefully as C. R. Rajagopalachari. The enforced incorporation of Kashmir into the Indian Union could not have been tolerated; and he would surely have fasted in protest against the ten years' incarceration of Sheikh Abdullah without trial. Would Gandhi have been prepared to buy friendship with China by acquiescence in the subjugation of Tibet? And if China had still launched an armed invasion of India, would Gandhi have accepted a nominal State of Emergency in India under which no real spirit of national regeneration is created? All these are speculations; but not unrelated to Gandhi's declared convictions. What is certain is that he would not have tolerated the continuing deterioration of relations between India and Pakistan which, by 1964, had reached their lowest point in mutual suspicion and bitterness, with the minorities and the refugees treated as little more than hostages and victims of intolerance. Gandhi's last fast was dedicated to relieving tension between India and Pakistan, and as an act of grace the cabinet led by Nehru was induced to hand over a large sum owing to Pakistan.[24] The years that have followed have been utterly barren of any act of Gandhian compromise and reconciliation on the part of the government of India.

[24] Tendulkar, Vol. VIII, pp. 259–60.

However, we must not conclude that (to cite one of the most delicious chapter headings invented by Tendulkar) we are left with "Swaraj Round the Bend".[25] A sense of dedication still pervades Indian politics and society. Much has been made of the failure of the Kamaraj plan for voluntary abjuration of office by the leaders of the Congress establishment. It has been said that the plan was utilised to remove those who had fallen out of favour at court, and that the consequences have been an intensification of faction. Even if there may be limited truth in this, the widespread readiness to relinquish power which was shown by ministers and chief ministers has no exact parallel elsewhere. It is necessary to recall Garibaldi's romantic self-exile, in order to find a similar gesture: a collective renunciation of power is unique.

Despite all the disillusioned gossip in opposition circles, the conduct of the 'Old Guard' of Congress politicians seems restrained by comparison with other countries in a similar phase of history. What do the charges of corruption add up to? Preferment for relations; trips abroad during a period of extreme currency shortage; directorships; honorary degrees; an abuse of official rules for travelling. But on the credit side, how much remains?

The administration, although liable to ministerial persuasion, remains extraordinarily free to conduct public affairs according to its own professional code. The opposition, though harassed occasionally, remains entirely free to criticise and oppose the government to the limit of its resources. The press and the courts of law, if they display independence, are not penalised or persecuted. The appeal to the people at elections, although attended by persuasion and a certain lack of favour to individuals or communities which withhold their support, is openly conducted; and defeat for government candidates is candidly accepted.

Many would claim other sources of inspiration for these freedoms, but the Gandhian influence is plain in the continuing awareness of the role of compromise and consensus in Indian politics. From all sides concern is voiced at what a communist MP described as 'political ding-dong'; the pursuit of political ends through disagreement. In Nehru's words: 'All our schemes and planning, our ideas of education and of social and political organisation, have at

[25] Tendulkar, Vol. VII, Ch. 6.

their back the search for unity and harmony.'[26] If the opposition asserts (with some reason) that Congress expects this search for harmony to proceed under the Congress umbrella, this is no more than was claimed by Gandhi and his colleagues in the days before independence.

Since 1959, a major step has been taken throughout India to revive Gandhi's 'dream of *panchayat raj*' in the new network of village and local councils which is called *panchayati raj*, or the 'reign of the village councillors'. This can lead to a revolution in rural life greater than any wrought by independence. For the first time since the Mughals consolidated their system of district administration (largely assimilated by the British) the locus of rural power has moved from the landlord and the high official to the rural community. The first consequence of the introduction of *panchayati raj* has been a struggle for the loaves and fishes among the dominant agricultural castes. But the ultimate end would seem to be the entry of the inert rural masses into the control of local affairs which has been denied to them since earliest times. And *panchayati raj* has come about through the realisation of tough party politicians that the only alternative to rural stagnation is a Gandhian programme of popular participation in community-building.

A leading part in this process has been played by persons outside politics and administration. For example, there is the Association of Voluntary Agencies for Rural Development, whose president is Jayaprakash Narayan, erstwhile militant socialist, now self-dedicated to the movement for *sarvodaya*. Among the more than fifty bodies brought together in AVARD, we may name at random the All India Women's Conference, the Shri Aurobindo Sevak Sangh, the India Village Service, Gandhi *Ashrams*, Grain Banks, the Seva Bharati School of Living, and the *Saksharta Niketan* or Literary House. All these are social-service groups devoted to rural uplift, quite outside the power struggle.

The outlook of this element in Indian life is given expression in the writings of Jayaprakash Narayan, notably *From Socialism to Sarvodaya* (1957), *A Plea for Reconstruction of Indian Polity* (1959)

[26] Illustrations of the search for consensus among Indian political leaders are provided in the present writer's *Ballot Box and Bayonet*, London and New York, 1964.

and *Swaraj for the People* (1961).[27] Just as Gandhi developed an original philosophy from his chosen sources of inspiration, so Jayaprakash is moving beyond the Gandhian view of political association. Yet, as he constantly acknowledges, his obligations remain. He writes: 'I still am an ardent believer, like Gandhiji, in the maxim that that Government was the best which governed the least. The test of human evolution for me became man's ability to live in amity, justice and co-operation with his fellow men without outward restraints of any kind. That is why I have considered the human and social problem to be at bottom a moral problem.'[28]

Because he believes in the urgent need to bring morality back into politics, Jayaprakash has espoused two of the least popular causes in contemporary India. He is working for reconciliation with Pakistan, and for the settlement of the Naga demand for independence. Early in 1964, the Muslims of Bihar and Orissa were the victims of communal brutality: allegedly, in retaliation against the persecution of Hindus in East Pakistan. In April, Jayaprakash and four of his fellow social workers issued statements, warning the Indian people against moral smugness. The sensational treatment of atrocities carried out in Pakistan in the reporting of the Indian press was contrasted with the suppression of similar incidents concerning Muslims in India: 'This has created an image in our minds that we are a very virtuous people who never engage in any unseemly acts.' A further statement went on: 'We believe that if the people of India come to know the truth about the monstrosities committed by our countrymen, their minds and hearts will revolt at it and they will be moved to make amends.'[29] At the beginning of September, Jayaprakash went to Pakistan in order to begin to create 'The ground for a new relationship of trust and confidence'; he also took part in the peace talks in Nagaland, and helped to bring about a cease-fire. The sequel to all this was that the man who might have succeeded Nehru, if he had remained in the mainstream of politics, aroused such a wave of emotional resentment that cries of 'Arrest him' and 'He must not be at liberty' were uttered in the Indian parliament.[30] One is reminded of the comment of a perhaps

[27] All published at Kashi (Banaras).
[28] *From Socialism to Sarvodaya*, p. 37.
[29] *The Times*, April 27 and 28, 1964.
[30] *The Times*, November 24, 1964.

not altogether biased Muslim leader on Gandhi in his last days: 'Having been relegated to the rank of a burdensome intruder in the affairs of the Hindu nation, his voice . . . fell on deaf ears.'[31]

Led by Vinoba Bhave, the followers of *sarvodaya* have put Gandhian principles into practice. Frequently they have failed. Yet also they have succeeded. Perhaps the greatest fascination in Indian politics today is not the perennial question of how the supreme struggle after Nehru will be resolved in the power-circus of New Delhi, but whether *panchayati raj* will acquire its own dynamic, and whether the principles of *sarvodaya* will gain that acceptance among ordinary men and women for which Gandhi longed: as it must have seemed to him, in vain.

Almost all those who stood alongside Gandhi in the national struggle have departed. One who remains to brood over the contemporary scene with rare detachment is C. R. Rajagopalachari. Here are his conclusions:

> What was Gandhiji's wish in respect of India after it became free and the people gained the opportunity of governing themselves? He desired simplicity in living to become a general feature. He desired self-sufficiency at least in food and clothing. He desired that the citizens should govern themselves freely and that the compulsory powers of the state should be reduced to the minimum. He desired Hindus and Muslims to live in mutual trust and fraternal amity. He desired firm friendship between India and Pakistan and elimination of all hostility between them.
>
> It is painful to go through these items one by one and to realise our failures in all these respects. . . . Indo-Pak amity is therefore the immemorial epitaph written on Gandhiji's Samadhi. Let us not cease to work for it. If friendship is achieved between India and Pakistan it will be a great and worthy memorial to the martyred saint. . . . If we do not work for this . . . homage paid to him would be hypocrisy.[32]

[31] Choudhry Khaliquzzaman, *Pathway to Pakistan*, London, 1961, p. 388.
[32] G. Ramachandran and T. K. Mahadevan (eds.), *Gandhi: his relevance for our times*, Bombay, 1964, p. 8.

10

East and West

REFLECTIONS AFTER A
GENERAL ELECTION OCTOBER 1964

GRAHAM WALLAS commenced *Human Nature in Politics* with the observation: 'The study of politics is just now [1908] in a curiously unsatisfactory position.' Were he writing in 1964 he would be even less satisfied. Poor man, he argued that 'the efficiency of political science, its power, that is to say, of forecasting the results of political causes, is likely to increase'. It would be interesting to hear Wallas's comments on the British General Election of 1964, when all the public opinion polls were confounded by the 'Don't knows', and when the political scientists of the BBC, backed up by batteries of computers and other mechanical devices, found themselves unable to forecast which party would win until almost the last constituency result had been declared. Perhaps Graham Wallas must bear some of the responsibility for the process whereby British academic studies of politics became absorbed in the mechanics of the political process and ceased to focus attention upon the meaning and movement of politics.

An altogether disproportionate amount of attention is given to the mechanism of elections. The concept of 'the swing of the pendulum', familiar since the nineteenth century, has been supposedly refined into a mathematical formula. At election time, personalities, policies and issues are all secondary to calculations of how the swing will affect the 'marginals', those constituencies which are held by a slender majority. In 1964, however heroic the struggle might be, however forcibly issues presented: unless the contest occurred in a 'marginal', it was not thought worthy of study by students of politics. As a result, although political science has become established in British universities quite broadly since the second world war, there is little if any advance in interpreting the political impulse in British life. One of the few studies of a British constituency is aptly entitled *How People Vote*.[1] *How* they vote— quite literally, how they cast their vote—with no attempt to discover, in depth, why they make up their minds to vote as they do, and under what influences and compulsions.

Asian political studies are, by comparison, becoming sophisticated and stimulating. The older conventional British approach to politics concentrated upon constitutional structure; and there is a large and somewhat leaden literature of a legalistic style concerning constitutional debate, constitutional formulae, and constitution-making in South Asia. During the 1950s, this legalistic approach gave way to the 'structural-functional' interpretation of politics. What this means, may be gathered by recalling the verdict of the German socialist, Karl Liebknecht, on the pre-1914 German Reichstag: 'a fig leaf to cover the naked absolutism of the Hohenzollern crown'. Academic students of politics began to 'take apart' the accepted structure of government, as it were, and to examine the different parts to see where power and influence actually resided. Many aspects of politics could not be explained in terms of parties or political ideologies. The roots of politics went deep into the soil of religion and the network of social relationships. Many social anthropologists began to extend their studies of village kinship into the field of politics.[2] Political scientists related their analyses of the politics of the state and the nation to the social framework. Perhaps of most significance was the coming together of sociologists and students of politics to examine the area of 'intermediary' politics: all that spectrum between the village and the capital, at local and

[1] M. Benney, A. G. Gray, and R. H. Pear, *How People Vote: a Study in Electoral Behaviour in Greenwich*, London and New York, 1956.

[2] For a particularly illuminating example of this mode of synthesis, see R. W. Nicholas, "Village Factions and Political Parties in West Bengal", *Journal of Commonwealth Studies*, Leicester, November 1963.

regional levels, where so much of the formative and executive processes of politics and administration are carried on.[3] Frequently, sociologists find it important to locate an institution in its historical context.

It may be argued that the Indian scene is specially rewarding for the structural-functional approach. The Indian tradition does not derive from any kind of theory of a Leviathan, a body-politic, as the necessary foundation for social action. Rather the Indian concept of *varnasramadharma*, the moral law of castes and classes and people, postulates government as an aspect of society. With the increasing intervention of the state in India, and especially the all-enveloping effects of centralised planning, the role of government may become dominant. It might be argued that in medieval Europe, religion and social custom were of greater significance than politics: and only because the nation-state became established at an earlier period do we attempt purely political interpretations. It becomes clear, as the European Economic Community begins to take over functions of the nation-state, that this form of international co-operation cannot be understood without reference to economic development, as well as to regional and historical variations of a non-political nature.

Most analysts of British politics share in the general insularity of their countrymen. They do not even begin to understand how the two-party system functions in the United States, with its manifold regional variations which arise from the social, racial and religious complexity of the great republic. It is unlikely, then, that they will be aroused by the suggestion that they might profit from considering ideas formulated within the South Asian context. However, to one who calls himself a contemporary historian, it is important to set down any observations which may assist to explain the meaning of the times. The theory of the two-party system in Britain today appears to depend upon the proposition that the individual voter can identify himself directly with a national party, with its nationwide array of candidates, and with its national programme. It is assumed that whichever party emerges with the largest number

[3] Contrast Myron Weiner's *Party Politics in India*, Princeton, 1957, in which caste and religion are barely mentioned, with his *The Politics of Scarcity*, Chicago, 1962, which is a searching analysis of political pressure stemming from social movements and social ferment in West Bengal.

of individual votes throughout the country has received a 'mandate' for its programme. The collective will of the nation is deemed to be represented by this almost random aggregation of individual votes, expressed in terms of support for a national party.

This, at any rate, is how an intelligent foreigner might assemble his theory of British politics by studying the British television and the British press for six months prior to a general election. Perhaps the first subject which British sociologists might investigate with profit is the extent to which the supposed atomisation of society has in fact proceeded. Is it true (as the Indian social philosopher, Jaya-prakash Narayan, has asserted) that the British electorate resembles a sandheap, 'a mass of disparate voters'? By comparison with the caste-bound society of India, this may be so. Yet to a surprising extent, Britain remains a *communitas communitatum*. Local, regional, even religious loyalties retain vestigial power, so that the link between the individual and the great society is by no means undifferentiated. Presumably this is conceded with regard to Scot-land and Wales, where there are quite significant tribal political parties, and where the national parties generally take care to select their candidates upon a tribal basis. Yet it is argued that in England the local, ethnic, or religious factors in a candidate's favour will sway only a few hundred votes, whereas the national, political appeal of the party and its leadership will pull in tens of thousands of votes.

Perhaps the reality is a little more subtle. Probably no local, or other personal appeal can do much against an adverse national, party-political trend. But the national parties pay more attention to purely local factors than is generally recognised.

If anywhere, it might be supposed that the outer London suburbs represent the sandheap; admass; an undifferentiated collec-tivity of unrelated individuals. The present writer has been able to study one such outer London constituency in detail. Although this constituency takes its name from an ancient market town, its boundaries follow largely arbitrary lines, to include—and to bisect—half-a-dozen different communities, with varying social structures. The average length of residence of a voter is about three years. Besides geographical mobility there is a great deal of social mobility; with 'working-class' people acquiring the standards of living of the middle class, and lower middle-class parents providing the spring-board for their children to attain professional status. Is it possible, then, to detect any sign of politics taking account of the community in such a melting pot? Personal observation suggests that it is.

The most striking example of this community-sensitivity occurred in the elections for the Greater London Council which preceded the 1964 General Election, taking place in April 1964. The 'Borough' sprawls even further from the eponymous medieval trading centre and staging post on the hill. This vast synthetic municipal abortion includes areas which have become the favourite residential choice of the middle-class and upper middle-class British Jewish *évolués*. These are second-, or third-, or tenth-generation British Jews, in terms of their evolution from the Warsaw ghetto, or even from the East End tenement. They come to reside in these pleasant semi-rural suburbs of London to shake off the last vestiges of the ghetto: their leaders claim that they are 'indistinguishable from the rest of the community'.[4] It is true that these assimilated Jews are an invisible community: unless, one special Friday evening, one drives unthinking through the dusk and suddenly discovers that at every street corner there are groups of men wearing identical trilby hats (or so it seems) who are quite distinct from the rest of the passers-by. All the national parties took note of this difference in their selection of candidates for the Greater London Council. None could afford to ignore the Jewish vote. The Conservative, Labour, and Communist parties each nominated one Jewish candidate (there were four seats to be filled). The Liberal party nominated two Jews among its four contenders. None of these Jewish candidates was an 'Uncle Tom', selected merely because he was a Jew: each had given years of service to his chosen party. Yet, his race or religion was certainly a factor in the process of choice.

The parliamentary contest for the same area in the 1964 General Election did not reveal such a direct interplay of forces. The present writer can only introduce more oblique examples of religious and social influence from his experience as Liberal parliamentary candidate. The connection between nineteenth-century Liberalism and Dissent is well-established. It might be supposed that the half-century, 1914–64, which witnessed such a complete change in the fortunes of both the Liberal party and the Nonconformist churches would have seen the withering away of this

[4] According to one councillor who exemplifies his own dictum.

connection. Certainly, the old, almost automatic active inter-relationship has gone; although the areas where the old Liberalism has survived all vicissitudes—especially the West Country—are mainly areas where Nonconformity remains a social force. However, even in an outer London suburb where the old Liberalism has been almost entirely submerged, and where the Free Churches exist like outposts in an alien land, the historic connection although apparently extinguished, even extinct, was in actuality only dormant, waiting to be revived.

Perhaps one-third of the Liberal parliamentary candidates in 1964 were Dissenters, mostly having a more than nominal church membership. In 1964 it was not clear that what might be called the inherited outlook would be relevant to the political role. Certainly, there was no attempt to utilise the local Free Church network for political motives. Indeed, the network did not appear to operate out-side the context of religion. For purposes of social pressure or action, local Nonconformity appeared to be not only invisible, but unidenti-fiable. However, the adoption of a Nonconformist parliamentary candidate did seem to bring about a certain transformation among many local Nonconformists from a passive to an active attitude to politics. Quantitatively this was not at first significant; but to an organisation which was attempting to establish branches in areas where there was no known tradition of Liberal activity, it was important to be able to inquire along a known network. Frequently the inquiry yielded nothing: but often it led to the adherence of one who was able to start the nucleus of a new organisation.

Now we may see the interconnection of Nonconformity and Liberalism in practice. The individual Free Churches are local, self-governing, self-supporting organisms. Any member is accustomed to giving generous individual financial support, and to participation in continuous fund-raising activities (bazaars, garden parties, etc.). He is used to regular attendance at church meetings, where manage-ment and planning are discharged. He is expected to have a thorough knowledge of his faith, and of its fundamental source, the Bible. Now, all this provides an inspired foundation for local politi-cal action: to a political party which is weak in funds and in profes-sional organisation, it provides a vital means of creating grass-roots organisation.

As the campaign got under way, so the invisible network of

Nonconformity (fragile, and representing a generation that is passing away, though it may be) seemed to establish an empathy with the Liberal candidate that was both personal and traditional. There was an impression that whereas a Nonconformist candidate of another political party would not have attracted a vote—and neither would a Liberal candidate who was not a Nonconformist have obtained a vote—yet when in this north London suburb a candidate appeared who symbolised two almost submerged traditions, old loyalties re-awakened. At the final meeting (the 'Eve of Poll Rally', as it was called) a BBC producer, who was filming the meeting for television, commented afterwards on what he called the 'warm feeling' and the active participation of the audience in all that happened. 'Is there a strong Free Church element in your support?' he asked. It was interesting that a complete stranger, who knew nothing of the local situation, should be able to identify one aspect of the sociology of our local Liberalism from its outward characteristics.

Group loyalty is still a factor in British politics; unrecognised, unidentifiable, sometimes; overt and assertive elsewhere. There are about one hundred British constituencies, all solid Labour strong-holds, where the nomination of the Labour candidate (and, auto-matically, the election of the MP) is the preserve of a powerful trade union. The role of groups needs to be investigated from many angles. Again, this has been much more fully worked out for contemporary Indian politics. In particular, Professor F. G. Bailey has shown that candidates for office in India make little attempt to appeal to the individual voter; they deal with 'brokers' who are able to draw upon what Bailey calls a 'vote bank', i.e. the block vote of a group, area, or class, which is conscious of a common interest, and is pre-pared to transfer the whole vote bank to the candidate most likely to promote their interest.[5]

Despite the oft-repeated assertion that the British electorate is ceasing to vote on class lines, the 1964 General Election provided plenty of evidence that automatic voting by the affluent to defend their comfortable, privileged position was matched by a hostile, anti-privilege vote by those who have not yet attained affluence.

It is part of the built-in advantage enjoyed by the two jugger-naut parties that they can draw upon vote banks, despite the current

[5] See especially F. G. Bailey's *Politics and Social Change; Orissa in 1959*, Berkeley, 1963.

fortune of the party; the strength or weakness, wisdom or folly, which might seem to condition its prospects. In a constituency which is not entirely imaginary, the Conservative party enjoys a vote bank of approximately 15,000. Thus: if, at a general election, the local Conservative organisation do no more than circulate a leaflet inscribed, 'Vote X, Conservative'—whatever may happen in the national political debate, whatever the public opinion polls may prophesy about the parties' rise or fall—when polling day arrives, 15,000 voters will, without exhortation or warning, record their Conservative votes. In the same constituency, the Labour vote bank is no more than 10,000, and no less than 8,000. The vestigial Liberal vote bank, after the vicissitudes of the last forty years, is 3,000 at most. Finally, there are some 25,000 voters in the constituency who cannot be regarded as forming part of any bank. This does not mean that they are floating voters: not at all: most of them would identify themselves by one of the party labels, if questioned. But these 25,000 will not poll automatically. They need some persuasion before they will stand up and be counted. Some are open to being persuaded to change their party allegiance. And some will not need much of an excuse to abstain from voting altogether. Therefore, the Conservative organisation has only to convince and to mobilise some 8,000 voters (probably all declared Conservatives, too) in order to ensure success. Labour would have to mobilise about 15,000 voters, above their vote bank, to capture the seat: while the Liberals would have to seek out, persuade, and cajole some 20,000 voters beyond the vote bank, before they could compete with the front runner. A local party organisation ought not to be judged so much by its total vote as by the number mobilised above the basic vote bank.

Political loyalty seems, to some extent, to be an aspect of locality. It would be expected that a municipal housing estate is, almost automatically, composed of adherents of Labour, and that a 'stock-broker' neighbourhood would be solidly Conservative. It is therefore perhaps not surprising that streets of small houses erected in the 1890s or 1900s prove to be residual strongholds of Liberalism. In part this is because the respectable artisans or clerks who bought their homes twenty or forty years ago are not of the type to move: but where these terraces are now occupied by a younger generation, something of the old political habits seems to be passed on with the house. Another distinctively Liberal type of area is the housing estate built in the late 1920s or '30s by a speculative builder; with semi-detached houses, three rooms upstairs, two downstairs. These were first occupied (probably) by ex-servicemen of the first world war, clerks or skilled mechanics: men who would not vote Labour, but who retained something of the 'Nation Fit for Heroes' spirit, a propensity to vote radical. Again, the voting habit seems to cling to the habitation. Perhaps the most interesting areas are those which are changing their social character: for example, a street of solid, well-built detached pre-1914 houses, once owned by 'city merchants', but not easily adapted to the servantless society. Today, the big houses are occupied by two families or are divided up into maisonettes. It is probable that almost every occupation and variety of social circumstance will be found in such a street. Here, because society is mixed and mobile, voting habits will also be fluid, and the 'floating voter', so often a fiction of the pollster, will be a dominant part of the pattern.

However, there are always areas which do not conform to any stereotype. For example, in the Division under discussion, there is at least one such area. Upon the nucleus of a rural village community there has grown up, in the last ten years, a pleasant semi-rural neighbourhood of detached, individual houses, occupied almost entirely by families under middle age of the professional or business-executive type. Such a neighbourhood might be expected to adopt a Conservative outlook in politics as an aspect of its social standing. There are, indeed, a large number of Conservative voters: but the old village and the new neighbourhood have returned Liberal councillors in local government, and demonstrated a degree of solid Liberal support at the general election.

This apparently atypical behaviour must be mainly ascribed to enterprising local Liberal leadership which, when the new estates were first occupied, was involved with, and identified with new forms of social activity and social service, and which helped to promote a local neighbourhood spirit.

Leadership is another aspect of politics which has been little studied by observers of British politics, but which already has acquired a sizeable literature in the field of modern Indian politics.

Contemporary studies of western politics, in so far as they investigate the theme of leadership, are almost entirely obsessed with Max Weber's concept of charismatic leadership. In the terms originally posed by Weber, charisma was a subject for exact definition: but the term is now invoked in all circumstances, whether it is applicable or not.

Leadership, as one sees it functioning in an open, democratic political party, is quite different from this stereotype of a *führer* and his following; leadership operates from within and among the ordinary mass of the party workers. This intermediary leadership has been analysed in the Indian context.[6] Frequently, distinctions are drawn between the 'front' leaders, the men who claim to have the following of the village folk, and the actual leaders who exercise influence without having to thrust themselves forward; and also between formal leaders—those who exercise power by reason of office (such as the headman)—and informal leaders who exert influence on a personal basis. These attempts at classification are equally appropriate to English local politics. But rather than cover the same ground, the present essay will suggest alternative ways in which leadership can be usefully assessed.

The first qualification which must strike the observer of local political organisation is that of the limit, or the level of leadership. Of very few active workers can it be said that 'the sky's the limit'. Almost everyone has an optimum level of effectiveness, after which his contribution falls away rapidly, or even takes on a negative quality. There are some persons who have a talent for organisation (or leadership or being a catalyst) within their own road, or square or tenement. Such people will create a sense of neighbourly co-operation and of purpose, based simply upon the simple, mutual relationships of those who share in the life of a street. As one such street leader said: 'I want to reach the point where, when I go down the street, everyone I meet feels that he has shared something with me, that we owe each other something. Then, at least, they will feel that they do owe me one thing: a vote on polling day.'

The next important level of organisation is that of the ward or the village. Here something more than neighbourliness is needed: an ability as a fixer, a reputation for energy and ability. The formula will vary. Then comes leadership at the district level, entailing a

[6] See R. L. Park and I. Tinker (eds.), *Leadership and Political Institutions in India*, Princeton, 1959, especially "Patterns of Influence within Rural India", by Evelyn Wood, which provides a systematic analysis of the *modus operandi* of local leadership.

good deal more: judgement, of men and measures, a reputation for integrity, and so on. But of course, these differences are more easily stated thus, artificially, in an academic analysis, than they are determined in the daily life of local politics. Because a person has done splendidly at the level of the street, there seems to be every reason to give him responsibility at the ward level. Because in a voluntary organisation there can be no laying down of orders, and no real supervision, the success or failure of the promoted leader is often realised only when the event is over: when the election is won or lost. There is no sure way of knowing whether a person will function effectively at the next level of leadership until the experiment has been tried. Education, personality, age, are not necessarily determining factors. Some local leaders are aware of their own limits. Many street leaders will conscientiously carry out their limited but vital role for years on end, not wanting anything more. Some ward leaders are content with the same purely local role. There was one superbly organised ward that may be cited, where the chairman —a man of experience, in politics and in business—steadfastly refuses to go beyond his ward: perhaps rightly, feeling that he has found the right milieu for his ability. More often, the capable ward leader is persuaded into taking on a wider responsibility too hastily.

Sometimes, unexpectedly, a man will find his right level in the wider context, having aroused some doubts about his suitability at an intermediate level. One such leader comes to mind: an entirely self-made man, who had fought his way up in business life from nothing, and had therefore acquired a somewhat aggressive personality, which gave him a reputation for being awkward, difficult, in the middle ranges of leadership. Yet, given the most difficult and taxing post in the constituency organisation, his true courage, his blazing energy, and his indomitable refusal to be beaten emerged for all to see. The awkwardness was forgotten (or forgiven) and the whole character of the man was transmuted by the challenge of the responsibility thrust upon him.

Another vital aspect of intermediary leadership is the extent of its durability. It cannot be assumed that persons who emerge as activists will—whatever their intention—take on the task and see it through to the end. Four main types of endeavour can be distinguished: the dynamos, the rockets, the squibs, and the winking lights. The dynamos are those few leaders who keep up the work continuously, maintaining the pressure themselves, and to some extent galvanising others into an effort beyond their usual capacity or will. But the number of dynamos to be found is all too few. Perhaps in an electorate of 60,000, a political party may be lucky enough to discover half a dozen. Very often, the organisation will mistake a rocket for a dynamo. The rocket also displays terrific energy and enthusiasm. The difference is that the rocket soars upward with dazzling brilliance; but within a short while its energy is spent, and there is nothing left. A voluntary organisation will often elect a rocket into a key position, on the strength of the first brilliance, only to find—too late—that for months after the first spasm of energy, nothing positive is happening. Only with experience does one learn to identify the rocket. But his febrile energy must not be rejected. The wise organiser gives his rocket some limited but important assignment to carry out; and then sees his man disappear, without rancour, and with gratitude for what he has achieved.

Sometimes it is not easy to distinguish a rocket from a squib. The latter is just a nuisance. He will turn up at committee meetings and pronounce an opinion with great force of conviction: but if the committee are sufficiently impressed to offer him a sphere of action, nothing whatever will come of it. The squib can exercise a negative power in the organisation, because of the noise he makes: but except as a trouble-maker his leadership qualities are null. The winking light is rather a contrast to all three preceding types of leader. In debate he is not especially convincing; in executive office, he is more noticeable for earnest intention than for determined action. But still, the winking light is a valuable element in the organisation. He will never galvanise others, as the dynamo does, into being greater than their usual selves: but he will keep going, more or less, for long years on end. He will provide the necessary infrastructure of leadership which is vital to local party organisation.

An accurate analysis of the forms of leadership and kinds of organisation peculiar to the different political parties is essential to understanding the differences in their character. These help to explain what kind of party the Conservative, Labour, Liberal or Communist label really covers. A party which claims to be open to all, to believe in equality of opportunity, and in the right of all members to have a voice in party counsels, ought to exhibit these attributes in its own internal constitutional machinery. If, within the party, decisions are made by a small cabal, or are determined by block voting, then the actual performance of the party on the national stage may be expected to reflect these internal characteristics, rather than its declared intentions.

It is true that students of British politics are likely to be confused by the ambivalent nature of the philosophies of the main parties in the 1960s. How far does the Labour party maintain a belief in socialism? And how far will any attempt be made to carry the definition of contemporary socialism beyond the hallowed ritual formula of 'the nationalisation of the means of production, distribution and exchange'? How far does the Conservative party have any coherent philosophy other than that 'The Queen's government must go on', having itself taken a hand in liquidating almost all its traditional symbols and beliefs? In the past, British politics has been nourished by the contributions of philosophers and publicists, by Oxford and Fleet Street. Where today are the successors of Cobbett or Coleridge? Academics seem to be almost wholly immersed in their own, highly technical linguistic philosophy, while journalism has become obsessed with the 'horse race' approach to politics. Once again, it seems to the present writer that those interested in the fundamentals of politics will find much more that is worthy of their study in Asia. The last section of this essay will be devoted to showing how the writer, in his attempt to participate in the public debate of British politics, has derived many of his ideas from modern Indian political thought.

For many years, the writer was a spectator of the political process. For one whose chosen life was that of the study, it seemed sufficient to observe the parties, their promises and their practices, and to exercise one's vote, so as to maintain a balance between the two major British parties, supporting whichever side seemed, at that time, to be least given to excess, or the lust for power, and most concerned to work towards a better society. Then came the Suez fiasco. The supposed checks and balances of the British constitution were seen to be inoperative. At the height of the crisis, a colleague— one normally content to pursue his own chosen specialisation in virtual isolation—rang up and asked 'What are we going to do about it?' What indeed? A petition of protest was circulated and signed and delivered to the prime minister. What was this but a gesture? The Suez affair revealed to the writer his utter helpless-

ness, as an individual, in what is regarded as one of the most democratic countries on earth. The root cause appeared to be the
perversion of the parliamentary system in Britain today. The system,
supposedly, is based upon four inter-communicating levels of
decision-making: the executive, parliament, the parties, and the
electorate. The electorate, the whole adult population, is supposed
to be sovereign, to decide its own destiny. The parties are supposed
to be the instruments whereby popular issues can be systematically
debated, and which provide responsible panels of candidates for
parliament: the parties give shape and direction to the representation of the many by the few. Parliament provides the context within
which the people's representatives can discharge their responsibili-
ties, and the executive forms the actual means whereby decisions are
implemented: but the executive is drawn from parliament, and is
responsible to parliament.

The Suez fiasco showed that the executive is the only one of
these four elements which counts, in terms of power. The electorate,
as individuals, are impotent to control events. Parliament may be
able to exercise the function of a sounding-board. The parties, in so
far as they are composed of individuals, are also helpless: but the
ruling party as the force which upholds the executive does exercise
immense power. If the party fractures apart (as at the fall of Neville
Chamberlain) then it surrenders power not to the individuals of
which it is composed, but to some new combination; another collec-
tivity of power.

The parties are supposed to be the pillars of democracy: but in
Britain, although we enjoy unqualified rights to set up and operate
political parties (and there are at least eight parties of national
significance), because of our electoral methods the choice for representation in parliament has been reduced to one of only two parties.
Is it far-fetched to suggest that a two-party set-up is a good deal
nearer to the one-party state than a multi-party system? Certainly,
by the middle 1950s, the two-party set-up at Westminster had
reached near-deadlock. No kind of development or movement was
possible within this set-up: as the negative reaction from both sides
to the challenge of western Europe was to show.

Yet contemporary British political writing barely seemed to
notice that there was a problem: and the only reform suggested was
the modernisation of the two juggernaut parties. In this situation,

an increasing number turned towards a 'third force' in British politics, the Liberal party. Many Liberals accept the general framework of the two-parties-in-parliament system, the Ins and the Outs; hoping to find a new dynamic from the emergence of a new Liberal, radical party to replace an ossified Labour party. This variation on the two-party ethos may have become accepted because, under present conditions, Liberals have been made aware of the helplessness of the individual, and therefore see a solution only in mass action, through the party. Also, as a healthy reaction against the retreat into the ivory tower of Liberals a few years ago, there arose an insistence that Liberals must not be afraid of power: they must seek to gain power, as a necessary step in the application of radical principles. It must be added that the Liberal concept of the open party allows individual members great freedom of decision; and that the Liberal concept of the working of parliament envisages a much looser party system, with much inter-party co-operation through a more sophisticated committee system. Still, the need for an alternative to the present polarisation of power has not been fully explored, even within Liberalism.

The most vigorous critical examination of the party system from a democratic point of view, known to the writer, is that of M. N. Roy. Roy passed most of his life as a communist; but having started as a liberal rationalist, he remained a thinker, and he was at last compelled to discard communism for its perversion, in practice, of its fundamental theses. Roy then evolved his own approach to social and political organisation through what he called a 'new humanism'. He aimed to transform democracy in its usual institutional form of parliament and parties into a partyless democracy.

Roy's view of the problem begins with the supreme importance of individual freedom:

It is the basic urge of all social advancement. Freedom is the progressive elimination of all the factors—physical, social, psychological—which obstruct the unfolding of man's rational, moral and creative potentialities. The function of social relationships should be to secure for individuals, as individuals, the maximum measure of freedom. The sum total of freedom actually enjoyed by its members individually is the measure of the liberating or progressive significance of any social order.[7]

Roy is writing mainly for an Asian audience. He is contemplating the new states which, in shaking off colonial rule, proclaim that in providing substitutes for freedom they are actually promoting a higher democracy; Roy is not impressed:

> A new world of freedom will not result automatically from an economic reorganisation of society. Nor does freedom necessarily follow from the capture of political power by a party claiming to represent the oppressed and exploited classes.... By disregarding individual freedom on the pleas of taking the fullest advantage of technology, of efficiency and collective effort, planned economy defeats its own purpose.... Economic democracy is no more possible in the absence of political democracy than the latter is in the absence of the former.[8]

Roy insists that 'politics cannot be divorced from ethics': he has parted from Soviet communism because 'the means have become the end'—which is dictatorship. He rejects the party system because the means nullify the end. If democracy involves the delegation of authority to a party, Roy sees this as the surrender of popular sovereignty. Here is his most forcible critique of the party system:

> Having reduced man to impotence, politics degenerated into a scramble for power between groups of people calling themselves parties. Though the party system is believed to be the essence of democracy, it has done more harm to democracy than anything else. It has reduced democracy to demagogy.... In all probability, those who make the big promises may really want to do good things. But engaged in the game of power they must play it according to its rules.... Degraded to the formality of counting heads, democracy does not bother what is in the heads. If the heads are empty of sense, the party getting the largest number of votes will have the largest amount of ignorance as its sanction.[9]

[7] M. N. Roy, *New Humanism; a Manifesto*, Calcutta, 1947. 2nd ed., 1961, p. 38.
[8] *Ibid.*, p. 39.
[9] M. N. Roy, *Politics, Power and Parties*, Calcutta, 1960, p. 192.

Roy's solution is to restore sovereignty to the individual voter. He insists that the politics of power must be replaced by the politics of freedom. This must involve a much greater participation by the people in their own government. Eventually, Roy foresees partyless democracy: but this, he acknowledges, may take a hundred years to achieve.

To the writer, as a prospective parliamentary candidate, all this rang true. After 1945, the independents and the small parties (such as the Independent Labour Party) disappeared from parliament. Decisions were increasingly imposed upon MPs, against their intellectual and moral judgement. Adherence to the party line in parliament was expected and enforced: as at Suez, and later over Britain's entry into the EEC. To work for the Liberal party was not to work for a take-over bid from Labour, but to emphasise the necessity for free alternatives to be effective in British politics.

If the ordinary elector was to be weaned from the horse-race attitude to politics, with his function limited to trying to pick the winner in a two-horse race, then he must be educated into regarding himself as having a positive role in the political process: he must become a participant, not a spectator. The Liberal party could never make a distinctive contribution by embracing bandwagon politics ('Join us: we are the winners') but must begin at the grass-roots by arousing the electorate. This was precisely the policy adopted by the Liberals. The election slogan 'Think for Yourself' was more than a gesture against catch-penny politics. It was a symbol of the attempt to create the politics of participation.

An election address is not a very permanent form of literature, but the opening paragraph of the writer's appeal to the electorate represents his considered approach to the dilemma of the times:

You have been told that the main issue in this election is modernising Britain. I am chiefly concerned about humanising Britain. This is the so-called Affluent Society. We are drifting into an apathetic society. When so much is glossy and new, our decisions are so often secondhand. The television tells us what to buy. The public opinion polls tell us what we think. Many of us work in vast concerns in which decisions are taken by remote control. Control of our government is most remote of all. MPs do not know what is happening, and even cabinet ministers are left in the dark when a new prime minister is chosen. Liberals intend to build a Britain in which ordinary people are participants, not spectators.

Participation: but how can this be achieved? Roy envisages the transformation coming only when power is handed back to the people, 'when a pyramidal structure of the state will be raised on a foundation of organised local democracies'. Roy wishes to see democratic instruments like the right of recall, and the referendum, brought into use. But he looks mainly to a change of heart: 'There must be a conscious and integrated effort to stimulate amongst the people the urge for freedom, the desire to rely upon themselves.'[10] Although westernised in outlook, Roy was at one with Indian philosophers—with Vivekananda and Gandhi—in believing that freedom derives not from institutional safeguards but from an inner spiritual awakening. This sense that liberty only emerges when the individual desires liberty, has been stressed by Roy's successor in promoting partyless, participating democracy, Jayaprakash Narayan. He declares:

> Democracy does not consist merely in its formal institutions. It lives, really and truly, in the life of the people.... It is not only through the representative assemblies and elected governments that democracy works, but in an equally true sense through the voluntary associations and actions of the citizens.... Professor Harold Laski, when asked how he would judge the worth of a democracy replied that he would do so by the amount of voluntary activity within it. Democracy has worked best among peoples that have shown initiative and enterprise.[11]

Jayaprakash goes somewhat further than Roy in searching for a dynamism which will make a reality of participation; this he hopes to find through social reconstruction.

> The problem of present-day civilisation is social integration. Man is alone and bored, he is 'organisation man', he is man ordered about and manipulated by forces beyond his ken and control—irrespective of whether it is a 'democracy' or dictator-

[10] *New Humanism*, 1961 ed., p. 43.

[11] Jayaprakash Narayan, *A Plea for Reconstruction of Indian Polity*, Kashi, 1959, p. 8.

ship. The problem is to put man into touch with man, so that they may live together in meaningful, understandable, controllable relationships. In short, the problem is to re-create the human community.[12]

Jayaprakash hopes to create a 'communitarian society', and part of the process will be the transformation of the politics of power and of the state (*rajniti*) into the politics of the people (*lokniti*). This he hopes to achieve through *sarvodaya*, 'the uplift of all', beyond party politics. To accept this point of view in its entirety would be to renounce any form of party association oneself. Jayaprakash mentions in passing that he 'toyed for some time with the idea of a co-operative, rather than a competitive system of parties', and he adds: 'I still believe that, given the psychological climate for it, such a political experiment might yet be made.'[13]

When the party is open, open to the influence of any member with something worthwhile to say, membership is a liberating rather than a constricting experience. The Liberal view of participating democracy involves a much greater range of active control over their affairs by ordinary people: through co-partnership in the firm, through a more complete system of education for a skilful society, through local and regional self-government. The Liberal approach also encourages the co-operative spirit in central government; through relaxation of the party whip, through a greatly-expanded system of specialist committees, and in general through the politics of debate and analysis, rather than through the politics of confrontation.

How far does this Liberal approach represent a way out of the present struggle for power? The aspect of the political philosophy of M. N. Roy and Jayaprakash Narayan which most would dispute is their contention that it is possible to transmute the politics of power into the politics of freedom: providing that the objective is not the concentration of power in the hands of a governing party, but the dispersal of power into the hands of the people, with political leaders working as the servants and not the masters of the people.

The Liberal in Britain in the 1960s was confronted with the

[12] *Op. cit.*, p. 37.
[13] Jayaprakash Narayan, *From Socialism to Sarvodaya*, Kashi, 1959, p. 36.

paradox that, in order to achieve the ideal of the dispersal of power and the participation of the people in the management of their affairs, it will be necessary first to obtain control over the source of all power: the central government. And yet—is this really the dilemma? Certainly, socialists have fallen into the trap of believing that socialism can only be attained through state control and state intervention.[14] Here again, Roy places the problem in its true perspective:

> People engaged in party and power politics cannot take a long view. Laying foundations is too long a process for them. They want a short cut. The short cut to power is always to make greater promises than others.... Therefore, the future of democracy in our country depends on people who are either outside politics today, or who will have the courage and vision to step out of the indecent scramble. They will have to act in a manner which may not attract the 'practical politicians'. They may have to plough a lone furrow for some time....[15]

One who protests against the two-party system must be prepared to work for long-term and not short-term objectives. This means a politics of faith, rather than the politics of works. Can a minority really exercise such a profound influence as to convert the ordinary people of Britain from the politics of apathy into the politics of participation? At times, it all seems quite baffling: never perhaps more baffling than after the General Election of 1964 when three million electors spoke with a Liberal voice—and found themselves virtually unrepresented in the new parliament. In this situation also, Roy supplies the key to fulfilment: 'When a man really wants freedom and to live in a democratic society he may not be able to free the whole world ... but he can to a large extent at least free himself by behaving as a rational and moral being, and if he can do this, others around him can do the same, and these again will spread

---

[14] In the work above, Jayaprakash cites from *Socialist Commentary*, July 1957, Jack Bailey, the British Co-operative leader, as saying: 'In Britain the concentration of most socialists upon the capture and use of state power has tended to blind them to the validity of non-state forms of socialism.'

[15] M. N. Roy, *Politics, Power and Parties*, p. 195.

freedom by their example.'[16] It is true that the classical Greek and Indian philosophers said this at the beginning; and it is true that in our age of tyranny, many have made this discovery again, all over the world. A man might find this truth from many sources. The writer of this essay found his understanding of the politics of participation from modern Indian thought. All the great problems of the world—racialism, fear of the other side, holding on to possessions, covetousness of others' possessions—all these problems exist within every man:

> *They cease not fighting, East and West,*
> *On the marches of my breast.*

The Kingdom of God is within you; Hell is within you; and at a lower level, freedom or servitude is within you. The man who knows that in liberating himself and those around him he is helping to liberate mankind, does not need to fear the big battalions.

Ex oriente lux. He who aspires to understand politics can learn much from a study of Asia, yesterday and today. One of the unexpected rewards of travel is the fresh vision, the new insight which is given to the traveller when he returns to his own native land. A man will often profit by lifting his eyes to new horizons before trying to understand what is immediately in front of him. But he must look for what really is; and not for what he expects to see.

[16] *Ibid.*, p. 196.

175